Performing and Performance: An Introduction
Heinz-Uwe Haus

Heinz-Uwe Haus

Performing and Performance
An Introduction

published through http://books.lulu.com/content/478806

Acknowledgements

I would like to thank the actors and collaborators, the students and faculty I have worked with during more than four decades at home and abroad, under professional conditions or in workshop situations, at guest assignments in theatre or academia or now for many years as permanent faculty at the Professional Theatre Training Program of the University of Delaware, whose willingness to challenge, along with their patience with my foibles, made my work possible.

I am immensely grateful to my son, Utz-Uwe Haus, who again managed to bring my notes into a proper form.

HUH

Preface

It is the aim of this collection of notes and comments to help the reader catch "the meaning of the business of the stage". This is not an easy assignment. What do we mean when we refer to the study of performing arts as "drama", "theatre" or "performance"?

This book does not reflect a coherent whole which springs from my head ready-made, but just the opposite. The study of and working on the stage – in the profession as well as in the academy – does not look for a final concept. Directing plays or teaching dramaturgy demands a dialectical dialogue as much between the art and the craft of theatre as between the interests of the spectator and the society.

The comments here are amendments and after-thoughts of an ongoing process to recognize and to look through some of the most relevant questions of performance theory and practice.

They examine the history and use of the professional terms and investigate the different philosophies, aesthetics, politics, languages and institutions with which they are associated.

The book analyzes changing attitudes to drama, theatre and performance over time. It explores the institutionalization of drama and theatre as university subjects, then the emergence of "performance" as practice, theory and as an academic discipline. It focuses on crucial terms such as action, alienation, catharsis, character, contradiction, empathy, event, fable, interculturalism, mimesis, presence or representation as "things to think about" and "things to do" as well. This way I try to stimulate fieldwork, classroom exercises and discussion.

The continuous challenge for grasping fundamental elements of performing is, that the minimum basic requisites for theater are flesh-and-blood actors confronting flesh-and-blood audiences. As one of my teachers at drama school always said: a play is born in a manuscript and buried in a printed text; it knows life, like a human being, only in a bright world of actions.

Each chapter provides tools of either specific training exercises and/or an analysis of their relationship to the practitioners' theoretical and aesthetic concerns. The central theme is the different concepts of identity represented by drama through-out the ages, whether political, religious, national, ethnic, class-related or individ-ual. The ideas explored within these texts examine the relationship between actor training and production and consider how directly the actor training relates to performance. They reflect a fact theatre makers since Thesbis were well aware of.

As a motto for this selection from my writing for students, teachers, practi-tioners, and academics as well, I choose Moliere's note [43] to the readers of a published version of his play *Love Is the Best Doctor*:

> *There is no need to tell you that many things depend entirely on the manner of the performance. Every one knows well enough that plays are written only to be acted; and I advise no one to read this unless he has the faculty, while doing so, of catching the meaning of the business of the stage.*

HUH

I Fundamentals

A dramatic plot will move before my eyes; an epic seems to stand still while I move round it. In my view this is a significant distinction. If a circumstance moves before my eyes, then I am bound strictly to what is present to the senses my imagination loses all freedom; I feel a continual restlessness develop and persist in me; I have to stick to the subject; any reflection or looking back is forbidden me, for I am drawn by in outside force. But if I move round a circumstance which cannot get away from me, then my pace can be irregular, I can linger or hurry according to my own subjective needs, can take a step backwards or leap ahead, and so forth.

(Schiller-Goethe correspondence, December 26, 1797)

1 What is up?

When a text is produced on stage, how is it received and interpreted by the spectator? This is a crucial issue for analysis of performances that use texts. In the Western tradition, the dramatic text remains one of the essential components of performance. In theatre it has long been assimilated as a primary component, with its performance on stage only accorded a subordinate optional role. Towards the end of the 19th century, however, things changed radically with the recognition of the director's function and the acknowledgement that a director is capable (or culpable?) of making a text produced on stage with the stamp of a personal vision. For the theatre of mise en scène, therefore, it is quite logical to focus analysis on the performance as a whole, rather than considering the latter as something derived exclusively from the text. Theatre studies, and performance analysis in particular, are interested in performance as a whole, in everything that surrounds and exceeds the text in an overall event. One repercussion of this has been the reduction of the dramatic text to the status of a sort of cumbersome accessory, now left rather contemptuously at the disposal of philologists. Within the space of fifty years, therefore, there has been a shift from one extreme to the other from philology to scenology.

2 Dramatic *versus* Epic

2 Dramatic versus Epic

plot	vs.	*narrative*
spectator is consumed	vs.	*is observing*
wears down will to action	vs.	*arouses will to action*
experience	vs.	*picture of the world*
spectator is involved in it	vs.	*must face it*
suggestion	vs.	*argument*
instinctive feelings presented	vs.	*bring to point of recognition*
spectator in thick of it	vs.	*stands outside of it*
status of being human taken for granted	vs.	*subject of inquiry*
mankind is unchangeable	vs.	*is changeable*
eyes on the prize	vs.	*eyes on the process*
one scene makes/leads to another	vs.	*each scene for itself*
growth	vs.	*montage*
linear development	vs.	*curves and loops*
evolutionary determinism	vs.	*jumps and skips*
wo/man as fixed point	vs.	*wo/man as process*
thought determines being	vs.	*social being determines thought*
feeling	vs.	*reason*

3

3 Theatre as a Transcultural Event

1. Don't accept what the dogmatists classify as absolute in the theatre.

2. Theatre and life are not absolute. Both are in a constant sate of flux.

3. Knowledge doesn't protect us from foolishness.

4. Doubters are in no way destroyers.

5. Through doubts we make discoveries.

6. Become masters of fate.

7. The audience needs to think as well as feel.

8. Re-examine tired aesthetics.

9. We must answer the question that Appia proposed, "How do we produce contemplated experiments?"

10. The process involved in creating theatre must be organic as opposed to spasmodic growth.

11. To move forward we must first look back.

12. As Grotowski says, "People who are dissatisfied create."

13. Resist what is normal in the theatre. Abandon rhetoric. Look towards the space beyond spoken language that is alive.

14. Choose process and collaboration rather than product and fragmentation.

15. The theatre is a place of social interaction. Have courage to e. Create a common vocabulary for an international realm.

16. Actors need to explore through their own experiences. They both willing and flexible.

17. Actors must develop their craft before pursuing a project.

18. In an ensemble, visualization makes discovery possible.

19. There are new laws formed every day. Don't take a one-way r granted because knowledge stagnates.

20. Truth is only asserted to the extent that we exert it.

21. We must develop a relationship between the past and the present able to progress. We must think universally.

22. A found solution to a social problem is merely a starting for a solution. It's a circle rotating through aesthetic enjoyment. This is what we mean by theatre to discover ourselves in our society.

23. Theatre as a social function has intensifies, especially in our third world countries. Dissatisfied fighting countries use theatre for revolutionary means. The theatre acts as an instrument of change.

24. The same production of a certain play takes on different meaning according to the society in which it is appearing. Thus, the theatre must be adaptable in order to create desired effects.

25. Transcultural theatre must be adaptable, truthful, derived from tradition and craftsmanship focused on communication of humanistic and universal principles, recognized as an arena for process and growth rather than an arena for product and stagnate absolutes and finally, it must speak to the children of our age.

References: Brecht, Grotowski, Appia, Shakespeare; The Greeks — Reinhardt, Meyerhold, Brook and Suzuki Technique

4 Thoughts to Steer by

Your own mental attitude is the one thing you possess over which you alone have complete control. When you set a goal – aim higher. Set your target and keep trying until you hit it. See beyond the routine.

When your energy level is low, the negative may subdue your health and your desirable characteristics. You are like a storage battery, your are dead when your energy level is zero. What is the solution? Recharge your battery? How? Relax, play, rest, and sleep!

How to tell when your battery needs recharging. Here is a checklist to help you determine your present energy level. You can use it whenever you feel that your energy level is slipping. If you are a well-balanced person your battery may need recharging when you act and feel. Unduly sleepy or tired, tactless, unfriendly, suspicious, querulous, insulting, hostile, irritable, sarcastic, mean, nervous, excitable, hysterical, worrisome, fearful, jealous, rash, ruthless, excessively selfish, excessively emotional, depressed or frustrated.

If your feelings actions indicate that those, are subduing your better qualities which are undesirable, and negative it's time to recharge your battery!

Yes, to maintain your level of both physical and mental energy you need to exercise both your body and mind.

5 The Narration of the Story by Grouping

Perhaps it is time to restore a little more equity and, if possible subtlety. My aim here is neither to return to a purely literary vision of theatre nor to engage in an endless discussion as to whether theatre constitutes literature of performance. Instead I propose to reconsider the place of text in performance and to distinguish between text as read off the page of a book and text as perceived as a *mise en scène*.

In this review of the principal elements of contemporary Western *mise en scène* and an attempt to conceive the most appropriate analytical methods for them, a select place should be reserved for the dramatic text – without however prejudging its status inside the performance. I conceived of the text as being within the performance rather than above or beside it. Most importantly, I aim to suggest a viewpoint and a method that are adequate to evaluate the impact and function of text within performance. Commentaries on dramatic texts only rarely take into consideration the ways in which they are manifested the individual reading of words in a book, or attendance at a live performance in the course of which the text is perceived most often delivered by the actors.

6 Rules of Thumb*

1. Read the play more than usual; don't jump into "living" the part;

2. Have a very clear idea of the *Grundgestus* — the political standpoint of the production;

3. When reading the play take a critical point of view of the character — question the character's actions and motives from a socioeconomic viewpoint;

4. Deal with each episode on its own terms; do not look for psychological consistency running through the play; look for the contrasts, the dialectic;

5. Look for choices of gestus that illustrate the overall gestus of each episode; the actor is not an individual but a part of a total scenic image;

6. In rehearsal the actor may explore every facet of a character, but must then make the choices of gestus in a socioeconomic context;

7. Keep a cool head in performance; don't be transported by the part or try to cast a spell on the audience — the audience's response should not be: "What a lifelike performance. I was quite carried away";

8. Know what critical response you would like the audience to have. It is the presentation of the character with a critical viewpoint that alienates emotional empathy.

7 The Use of Transitive Verbs for Playing Actions

Aristotle defined action as the energy driving a play or a scene. It is the central tool for story telling. For our training purpose we focus on action as a movement of will. It can be connected to physical activity, but its function is to provoke an inter-action with the other(s) on stage, creating a situation. It is a purposeful doing directed toward an objective. By asking your emotional memory for transitive verbs, your ability to imagine a situation, to "see" it in the mind's eye, allows you

---

*Excerpt from the dramaturgical material for a *Richard III* production at University of Guelph, Ontario, Canada, winter semester 1983.

to respond to your mental image. That response is always a narrative action, telling the spectator what the performer is doing to achieve his goals.

A strong action expresses vividly an emotional state, but does not call upon the actor to "play" emotions. An action is expressed as a verb, "to _____," not as "to be _____." Example: "To be sad" is vague and encourages the actor to try to summon an emotion on cue; "to mourn" is specific and playable, as are "to grieve" or "to lament."

A strong action expresses subtext and encourages interesting, concrete choices. Example: "to inquire" is general and weak; "to probe," "to harass" or "to finagle" are strong forms of inquiry, which specifically express a situation or relationship.

Actions in relation to other are also called tactics; tactics are analogous to directions of physical movement. In relating to others, we may move toward them or away from them, and position ourselves below (submissive to) or above (superior to) them. We may move obliquely – side to side – or plant ourselves firmly I one spot. Though actions are not always directly expressed through the direction of physical movement, using this analogy can be helpful in finding the strongest action. Thus, action verbs can be generally classified as follows:

Action Classification	Direction of Movement
aggression	toward and above
approach	toward and below
rejection	away and above
retreat	away and below
avoidance	side to side
vacillation	side to side
standing pat	planted

Actions in relation to ourselves express emotional or intellectual processes and generally don't have a consistent directionality.

Classifications are a convenience, but it should be noted that many actions may fall into more than one category: "to ridicule" is usually a rejection but may also be used as an attack; "to entertain" is usually an approach but may sometime be avoidance.

The following list contains action verbs roughly classified as above. The list is intended as a resource and a stimulus to imagination.

Actions

Aggressive

abuse	ax	bully	cross-examine	erupt
accost	backbite	bushwhack	crowd	escalate
admonish	badger	capture	crush	evict
advance	bad-mouth	castrate	curse	explode
affront	baffle	censor	damn	exploit
aggravate	bait	challenge	dare	expose
agitate	bamboozle	charge	debate	fabricate
alarm	ban	chase	defeat	face
ambush	banish	chastise	defend	fluster
anger	bar	checkmate	defy	foil
annihilate	barge	chide	delay	forbid
annoy	bark	claim	demand	force
antagonize	battle	clamp down	demolish	frighten
appall	beat	claw	demoralize	gall
apprehend	bedevil	clobber	destroy	goad
appropriate	belabor	coerce	devour	grapple
argue	berate	command	dictate	grill
arise	besiege	compel	discipline	gripe
arm	blast	compete	disgrace	grouse
arouse	bludgeon	complain	dispute	halt
arrest	bluff	confront	disrupt	hammer
assail	blurt	connive	dog	harangue
assault	bluster	conquer	dominate	harass
assert	boast	conspire	dress down	harm
astonish	bombard	contend	drill	harp at
attack	boss	contest	drive	hassle
attest	bother	contradict	dupe	hate
avenge	brag	counter	egg on	heckle
aver	brave	counter-	emphasize	hinder
avow	buck	attack	enrage	hiss
awaken	bug	crack down	entrap	hound

9

hustle	misdirect	police	stifle	twist
impose	mislead	pose	sting	tyrannize
incite	molest	pounce	stop	undercut
incriminate	muster	preempt	strafe	undermine
inflame	nag	press	straight arm	unmask
infringe on	nail	prick	strike	unnerve
infuriate	needle	prod	stun	unsettle
inject	negate	provoke	stupefy	upbraid
injure	object	pulverize	subjugate	usurp
inspect	obstruct	puncture	subvert	vanquish
insult	offend	push	surmount	vex
interfere	oppose	rankle	surpass	victimize
interrogate	oppress	rap	swagger	vie
interrupt	order	rattle	terrify	vindicate
intimidate	oust	rebut	terrorize	wallop
intrude on	outshine	reprimand	thrash	warn
invade	outwit	repudiate	threaten	weasel
investigate	overcome	repulse	thrust	whack
irk	overpower	retort	thwart	wheedle
irritate	override	rip	topple	whitewash
jab	overrule	scare	toss	whore
jolt	overrun	scold	toughen	win
jostle	overshadow	scorch	tousle	wither
jump	overthrow	shatter	trample	wound
lash	overwhelm	snap	transcend	wrangle
lecture	persist	snarl	traumatize	wrestle
libel	petrify	spar	trespass	zap
loom over	pierce	squelch	triumph	
madden	pin	stab	tromp	
manipulate	plunder	stalk	trounce	
menace	poke	startle	tussle	

Approach

absolve	accept	acclaim	accommodate	acknowledge

acquaint	bolster	confide	engross	greet
adapt	boost	congratulate	engulf	guide
administer	bribe	conjure	enjoy	gush
admire	brighten	console	enlighten	haggle
adore	broach	consult	enrapture	hail
advertise	broadcast	convince	entertain	hasten
advise	bubble	coo	enthrall	hawk
advocate	burble	cooperate	entice	help
affirm	buttonhole	corroborate	entreat	hint
aid	cajole	counsel	envelope	hold forth
amuse	calm	cradle	exaggerate	honor
announce	campaign	crave	exalt	hook
anoint	canonize	crusade	excite	hover
appeal	captivate	cuddle	excuse	humor
appease	caress	dazzle	exhort	hypnotize
applaud	caution	declaim	explore	idealize
approve	champion	delight	extol	imitate
assist	charm	delve	eye	implant
assuage	chat	dicker	fall for	implore
assure	chatter	disarm	finagle	imply
attend	cheer	disclose	flatter	impress
award	cherish	dissuade	flirt	include
baby	clasp	divulge	follow	infatuate
back	cleave to	dote	fondle	infect
banter	cling	dramatize	forgive	inflate
bare	clown	ease	fortify	influence
bargain	coax	electrify	foster	ingratiate
barter	coddle	embrace	free	initiate
becalm	collaborate	enchant	galvanize	insist
beckon	comfort	encircle	gibe	inspire
bedazzle	commend	encourage	give	instigate
beg	commit	endear	glamorize	instill
beseech	compare	endorse	glorify	instruct
bewitch	compromise	enfold	gossip	intercede
bless	con	engage	gratify	interest

intervene	milk	pity	reveal	testify
interview	mirror	plead	revere	thank
intoxicate	mollify	please	romanticize	tickle
intrigue	moralize	pledge	rouse	tiptoe
introduce	motivate	preach	scintillate	titillate
invest	mystify	preside	scrutinize	
invigorate	negotiate	prime	seduce	toast
invite	nestle	prize	serve	touch
involve	notice	probe	smother	tout
jest	nourish	profess	snoop	trail
join	nudge	prompt	snuggle	transport
joke	nurse	propose	socialize	treat
justify	nurture	protect	soft soap	tug
kibitz	oblige	pry	solicit	tweak
kid	offer	psychoanalyze	soothe	unarm
laud	open up to	puff	steer	
lavish	orate	pull	strengthen	unburden
lead	ordain	pump	subdue	unify
lean on	over praise	pursue	suffocate	unveil
leer	overprotect	ratify	suggest	uplift
level with	overrate	ravish	supplicate	validate
liberate	pamper	recommend	support	volunteer
lift	pander to	recruit	surprise	vouch
love	pardon	rectify	suspect	vow
lure	penetrate	regale	swear	welcome
lust after	perform	relieve	sympathize	
massage	persuade	remind	tantalize	whet
meddle	petition	repay	tempt	worship
mediate	pitch	rescue	tend	

Rejection

abandon	abrade	back out	belittle	burn
abolish	alienate	balk	besmirch	bury
abominate	ape	begrudge	betray	castigate

chafe	despise	distance	invalidate	prohibit
condemn	detest	distrust	jeer	rake over
condescend	detract	doubt	jilt	rebel
criticize	diminish	eject	judge	recoil
debase	disapprove	embarrass	knock	reject
decline	disavow	envy	leave	relegate
decry	discard	exclude	malign	repel
defame	discharge	finger	mimic	resent
deflate	disclaim	flaunt	minimize	rid
degrade	discount	fool	mistrust	scoff
deign	discourage	forsake	mock	sever
demean	discredit	gloat	mortify	slash
denigrate	disdain	harden	neglect	smear
deny	disillusion	humiliate	obfuscate	smirk
deplore	dismiss	ignore	ostracize	sniff
deprecate	disobey	impugn	patronize	snort
deride	disown	insinuate	persecute	taunt
desert	disparage	intimate	plot	welsh

Retreat

abscond	collapse	elude	pacify	succumb
accede	comply	escape	permit	tattle
acquiesce	concede	fall back	quit	thaw
admit	condone	fall flat	recede	tire
allow	conform	fear	regret	tremble
apologize	consent	flee	relent	weary
assimilate	cop out	flinch	relinquish	whimper
atone	cower	forfeit	resign	whine
back away	crack	give in	retract	wilt
back down	crawl	give out	retreat	wince
back off	creep	give up	scramble	withdraw
backpedal	cringe	hide	settle	yield
bemoan	crumble	intellectualize	shrink	
budge	defer	lag	shrug	
capitulate	drop back	melt	simper	
cease	drop out	obey	submit	

Avoidance

avert	dawdle	divert	feign	sulk
avoid	deflect	dodge	forestall	
block	digress	duck	pout	
conceal	dillydally	evade	rationalize	
dally	distract	fake	sidestep	

Vacillation

babble	fluctuate	quibble	stammer	vacillate
equivocate	fumble	ramble	straddle	waffle
fiddle	grope	shift	swerve	wander
fidget	hedge	shudder	teeter	waver
flail	hem	shuffle	totter	wriggle
flounder	hesitate	squirm	twitter	yammer

Standing Pat

abide	clam up	hold out	stand pat	withhold
absorb	cope	reconcile	stipulate	withstand
abstain	endure	resist	suppress	
await	freeze	resolve	temper	
ball up	gird	restrain	tolerate	
brace	hold to	stand ground	weather	

Intellectual processes

analyze	deduce	foresee	realize
comprehend	deliberate	gauge	reckon
compute	dissect	infer	surmise
consider	figure	plumb	weigh

Emotional processes

agonize	anguish	anticipate	bask	beam

bereave	droop	grumble	ponder	stew
bridle	effervesce	hallucinate	pray	suffer
bristle	effuse	hope	pretend	sweat
brood	enthuse	hunger	puzzle	swoon
browse	envisage	imagine	radiate	tighten
carouse	expect	lament	reflect	toil
cavort	exult	languish	rejoice	wallow
celebrate	fantasize	long	reminisce	wish
crow	fret	mourn	revel	wonder
daydream	fritter	mull over	rhapsodize	yearn
despair	frolic	use	ruminate	
discover	fume	palpitate	seethe	
dread	fuss	panic	sizzle	
dream	grieve	plan	smolder	

Finally a reminder about the role of the audience in this search for playing actions. Actors have to trust, that the audience understands the story by observing their actions. Theatre derives characters from their actions. And the actions are unfolding a play's events. For the actor to be "in action" is to be totally involved in the task at hand, but it also means to refer to the audience's storage of stories. And that puts him in the position to make choices, what to play or not to play. The purpose of rehearsals in not (only) for refining the technical presentation of an action, but more for finding ways and means to make the story easily narrated and to bring out its social significance. The actors and the audience's emotional memory are from the same social reality. The use of transitive verbs for playing actions encourages finding out what socially valuable insights and impulses the play may offer.

8 Rehearsal Techniques in Brecht's terms*

Brecht himself suggested various ways to approach epic ("story telling") acting:

    1. transposing the actions and remarks of the character into the third person

---

*Quotations from Bertolt Brecht, *Schriften zum Theater IV* [4, pp. 51–52].

2. transposing the action into the past

3. speaking the stage directions

Thus, a piece of action in rehearsal might go as follows: "Mother Courage slowly got down from her wagon, walked over to the officer, looked at him and said..."

Using the third person and the past tense enables the actor to achieve the right attitude of distance from the action. Putting the action in the past allows the actor to look at the words and make judgments on them. Speaking the stage directions in the third person has the effect of alienating them from the text itself.

These techniques may be varied and elaborated upon. The stage manager can call out the stage directions or narrate the action as the actor moves through it: "so then Mother Courage wearily sat down, took her daughter Katrin's hand and waited for the soldiers to bring in the stretcher bearing the body covered with a sheet." The actor may use the third-person alienation technique and add a comment upon the action — the kind of critical comment that the gestus should convey: "He stood up weakly, as due to the soldiers taking the food, he had not eaten for three days and facing the officer with bitterness said ..."

As basic model for an Epic Theatre stands Brecht's note on the *Street Scene*. The notion of the man at the street-corner miming an accident is also in *Theaterarbeit*, *Versuche 14* and *Gedichte 3* developed at length, and it also occurs in the following scheme, which may relate to lessons given by Helene Weigel at a Finnish theatre school:

Exercises for Acting Schools

(a) *Conjuring tricks, including attitude of spectators.*

(b) *For women: folding and putting away linen. Same for men.*

(c) *For men: varying attitudes of smokers. Same for women.*

(d) *Cat playing with a hank of thread.*

(e) *Exercises in observation.*

(f) *Exercises in imitation.*

(g) *How to take notes. Noting of gestures, tones of voice.*

(h) *Exercises in imagination. Three man throwing dice for their life. One loses. Then: they all lose.*

(i) *Dramatizing an epic. Passages from the Bible.*

(j) *For everybody: repeated exercises in production. Essential to show one's colleagues.*

(k) *Exercises in temperament. Situation: two women calmly folding linen. They feign a wild and jealous quarrel for the benefit of their husbands; the husbands are in the next room.*

(l) *They come to blows as they fold their linen in silence.*

(m) *Game (k) turns serious.*

(n) *Quick-change competition. Behind a screen; open.*

(o) *Modifying an imitation, simply described so that others can put it into effect.*

(p) *Rhythmical (verse-speaking with tap-dance).*

(q) *Eating with outsize knife and fork. Very small knife and fork.*

(r) *Dialogue with gramophone: recorded sentences, free answers.*

(s) *Search with 'nodal points'.*

(t) *Characterization of a fellow-actor.*

(u) *Improvisation of incidents. Running through scenes in the style of a report, no text.*

(v) *The street accident. Laying down limits of justifiable imitation.*

(w) *Variations: a dog went into the kitchen. (A traditional song.)*

(x) *Memorizing first impressions of a part.*

Brecht's so-called theoretical works are full of such very practical descriptions and notes to clarify and train his method. There is not such thing like a "Brecht theory." Instead one can experience in his theoretical writings a way of viewing the reality, encouraging the narrating and "dialectizing" of events. Even the most condensed literary paragraphs (as in the "Organum") or the specially created terminology (from "Alienation Effect" to "Social Gestus") are for the kind of theatre aimed at and to a large extend practised by Brecht and his pupils for more than three decades. Their revolutionary impact on the development of theatre arts is obvious worldwide. For English speakers I suggest to study John Willett's edition of "Brecht on Theatre" [58], where one can find the instruction, knowledge and enlightenment Brecht stands for. On less than 300 pages all essential thoughts, training techniques, and aesthetic goals can be discovered within their dramaturgical contexts and professional solutions. Teaching by learning was one of Brecht's rules of thumb, which Brook, Strehler and Stein, just to mention a few masters of post-Brecht Western theatre, made into a common strategy for their theatre work.

9 The necessary skills and talents of the director

- A concern for socially valuable insights and impulses the play offers

- A visual sense

- A rhythmic sense

- The ability to discover contradictions in human behavior

- The ability to analyze dramatic structure as story telling

- The ability to translate the main episodes into positions and movements

- The ability to interpret through image and metaphor

- The ability to work with actors

- Strong managerial skills

- Physical stamina

- Discipline

10 Brecht: Phases of a Production*

Analysis of the Play
Find out what socially valuable insights and impulses the play offers. Boil the story down to half a sheet of paper. Then divide it into separate episodes establishing the nodal points, i.e. the important events that carry the story a stage further. Then examine the relationship of the episodes, their construction. Think of ways and means to make the story easily narrated and to bring out its social significance.

First discussion of the setting
Basic idea of the set. Will a permanent set do the trick? Settings for individual scenes or acts. Creation of stage sketches which supply elements of the story, groupings, individual attitudes of the chief characters.

---

*following Brecht's suggestions in *Theaterarbeit* [2, pp. 63-64].

Casting

Preferably not irrevocable. Allow for the actor's need to be given a variety of roles. Avoid theatrical convention wherever it contradicts reality.

Reading Rehearsal

The actors read with the least possible expression and characterization, chiefly to acquaint themselves with the play. Distribute the analysis.

Positioning Rehearsal

The main episodes are roughly and provisionally translated into positions and movements. Various possibilities are tried out. The actors get a chance to test their own notions. Emphases, attitudes and gestures are roughly indicated. The characters can begin to emerge, though without any attempt at continuity.

Set Rehearsal

The experience of the positioning rehearsals is used to transfer the designer's sketches to the stage, so that work on them can start right away; for the sooner the actor can perform in the completed sets the better. From now on everything essential to the acting must be provided in a form fit for use (walls, flats, doors, windows, etc.). Nor should there be any rehearsing without props.

Rehearsal of details

Each detail is rehearsed individually, ignoring the final tempo. The actor builds up his character's attitude to the other characters and gets to know what he is like. Once the main episodes are more or less in shape the linking passages are rehearsed with special care.

Runs-through

Everything pulled apart during rehearsal of details is now pulled together again. It isn't a matter of tempo but of continuity and balance.

Discussion of Costumes and Masks

Once the groupings can be seen as a whole and the characters emerge individually then costumes and masks are discussed and work on them begins. High heels, long skirts, coats, spectacles, beards, etc., have already been tried out experimentally in the early rehearsals.

Checking Rehearsals

A check to see whether the play's socially valuable insights and impulses are getting across, whether the story is being fully and elegantly told, and whether the nodal points correspond. It is now a matter of probing, inspecting, and polishing.

Tempo Rehearsals

The tempo is now decided. Length of scenes is settled. It is as well to conduct these rehearsals in costume, as this slows matters down.

Dress Rehearsals

Runs-through

The play is run through very rapidly without a prompter. Gestures are indicated.

Previews

To test audience reaction. If possible the audience should be one that encourages discussion, e.g. a factory or student group. Between previews there are correction rehearsals, to apply the lessons learned.

First night

Without the producer, so that the actors can move without feeling they are being watched.

II Rules of Conversation

Commanding, entreating,
Relating, menacing,
Interrogating, answering ...
Belong ... to the art of
acting.

(Aristotle, The Poetics)

11 To Start With

1. What is said and done on stage must be seen and heard by the audience. The simple requirements of audibility and visibility form the basis of numerous stage conventions and techniques, but before we care about them, establish a "dialogue" with the spectators, "speak where they are" not around yourself. You are a storyteller you "en-act" in the mind of the audience the situations you describe.

2. Related to the problems of audibility and visibility are the instruments of expression themselves, the voice and the body. The value of a free, responsive voice and a rhythmic, expressive body cannot be overemphasized. How to develop such a voice and such a body is another matter.

3. It is focus, control, and coordination of energy that count, not an absence of energy. Some help toward gaining a free, expressive body may be found by returning imaginatively to the uninhibited, expressive day of childhood. Copying other people is a basic acting training tool.

4. Freedom in use of the body may also be gained from athletics and dancing, but whatever the technique, the objective to strive for is a body that without strain or affectation expresses feelings and ideas, not just with the

face muscles, not just with the voice, not just with the hands, but with the coordinated power of the entire body.

12 The Actor Should

1. Read the play more than usual; don't jump into "living" the part, "wonder" about contradictions in events and behavior.

2. Have a very clear idea of the basic attitude of the actions you demonstrate.

3. When reading the play, take a critical point of view of the

   character — question the character's actions and motives from a socioeconomic viewpoint. Try out different transitive verbs to free your mind for contradictory attitudes.

4. Deal with each episode on its own terms, do not look for psychological consistency running through the play; look for the extreme contrasts, the dialectic.

5. Look for choices of gestus that illustrate the overall gestus of each episode. The actor is not an individual, but a part of a total scenic image. All on stage narrates your story.

6. Enjoy by focusing on different ways of interpreting a character's actions. How the spectator changes into a critical observer who must make decisions how he finds "use value" in your demonstrations.

7. Keep in mind: the "emotional memory" of the audience finds its interest in observing your performance. They read with their eyes and imagining with their mind what you are telling them. They listen to you to feed their playground.

13 How to interact

Without the mutual openness and reciprocity of sharing that are the marks of theatre training the academy and the classroom become flat and impoverished –

reverting to collections of individuals, not communities of learning. To structure academic classes like theatre rehearsals, each participant talents and skills, his distinctive experiences have to become resources to start with. As a result, the various competencies attempted to promote take root in the individual's own identity. Students in my academic classes know from the very first day, that each member of the newly created community of learners is a resource for the other. Each give s others the right to place a claim upon some of the individual's time. In working groups of 3 to 5 participants they are responsible for creating projects on the base of "field observations", training their ability to relate their studies in class to social reality. Presentations in class focus on diverse "excavations" and enlighten to accept contradictions as a basic tool to look for the contrasts, the dialectic, not the psychological consistency running through a play.

An engaging metaphor for this kind of ethos is "conversation". David Tracy summarizes what it might entail: "A game with some hard rules: say only, what you mean; say it as accurately as you can; listen to and respect what the other says, however different or other; be willing to correct or defend opinions if challenged by the conversation partner; be willing to argue if necessary, to confront if demanded, to endure necessary conflict, to change your mind if the evidence suggests it."[56, p. 19]

The metaphor of conversation also says something about authority. The practical rules of theatre — to be in time, to be prepared, to be committed, to mention just a few — create conditions of discipline for team work as well leadership. Working to assure others, and oneself, that the class is moving toward (rather than away from) the announced goals and learning objectives means that one simply cannot withdraw from a position of authority. But authority needs the strengths of the instructor, which will be the base for trust, a fiduciary responsibility for advancing the creativity of the student. As the director in a rehearsal the instructor of a class has to use his strengths in the service of the participants learning. "Conversation" encourages to "fabulate" and to model social events into human behavior and actions.

14 Observation and Fable*

In a directing seminar at the University of Delaware in spring 1997, undergraduate students studied Brecht and some of his influences on theatre making. The students discussed the provocative nature of epic theater and its promotion of the potentially fearful prospects of unfettered thought and new ideas. Then, putting study into practice, they experimented with mediation and observation of fables. The first exercises in mediation involved the fable of Arturo Ui. First, students created headlines for the individual scenes of the play; then, they built parodies of poems to retell the fable. These new retellings exposed connections to western intellectual traditions previously unobserved in the classroom.

Choosing a familiar form, like those poems, allowed the students to mediate the fable very differently from Brecht's text. Students were able to focus on the process of mediation and discuss their choices. The serious practice began with a field observation. Students received instructions to go out of the academy and find a fable. The results yielded stories from the Division of Motor Vehicles, a gambling house, Renaissance Italy, and a school office in Chicago. The work done finding alternate perspectives and — interpretations of the Ui fable made it possible to find alternate ways of viewing these situations.

Here three examples:

Susan K.'s poem is modeled on A. E. Houseman's verse, *"As into the Garden Elizabeth Ran."* Her comment: "I choose this poem to emphasize the contrast between the content of the fable and the nursery rhyme-like quality of the verse. The original also displays this type of tension as the reader discovers dead frogs and sibling strife in a pleasant sing-song poem."

> As Into Corruption Old Dogsborough Flew
>
> As into corruption Old Dogsborough flew,
> Haunted by doubts that nobody knew,
> He took on an offer that lay in his lap,
> He took on an offer that in truth was a trap,
> And after supporting Big Ui's latest racket,

---

*Some student exercises presented at IMISE conference, Naples, Italy, July 15–21, 2000, and in[19].

26

He looked like a man who just couldn't hack it.

As one after another the witnessed died,
They knew of the docks, and they tried to hide,
One shady blaze burned a warehouse to bits,
The unlikely culprit was one Mr. Fish.

Behind all the drama sat plotting Arturo,
His intrigues and dealings always so thorough,
Biding his time and choosing his path,
Killing his foes and his friends, at the last.
All to the end of extending his power,
This tale of ambition gone somewhat sour.

Maureen E. C.'s poem is based on the Gaelic poems of Nuala Ni Dhomhnaill. These poems consist of storytelling and sing-song rhymes.

The Race to the Rise

This was the year that suspicions grew
for the Cauliflower Trust was never true.

Innuendo and conjecture were all around
but no concrete evidence was ever found.

The witnesses remained silent,
while the Trust grew violent.

The first victim was barely of age,
and now murder has set the stage.
As the small man continues his ascent,
the grocers begin their rapid decent.

In the middle of the night ghosts haunt and taunt
this little man, because his emotions no longer can.

He seeks solace in places that are familiar to him,
evoking God's name with a hymn.

But in the end none of us are free,
because of Arturo Ui.

His troops have expanded beyond and the taking of
Cicero has confirmed this mighty con.

Brandon Sch.'s poem is styled after a montage of T. S. Eliot's *"The Wasteland,"*
"Love song of J. Alfred Prufrock," and *"The Hollow men."*

Unreal City

Pockets full of holes
green lake, wide observer, sitting at a distance
reflect our mind's pieces, give peace back.

Eulogeses: don't hold your breath,
the smell isn't that bad
(fish out of water, fear death by starvation)

Pockets full of holes, trading Trust
for all our peaces, sifting dust
and 30 cent pieces
an old hamlet dog nose a rat a rat,
a rat-tat-tat   "dead for a daggot"

...but guns call forth no tears, only
dust here,
"Here will I show you fear..."
...in this hand, I deal
choice is no choice (this card predicts)
behind veils of peace
lie machine gun pieces and other fabricated truths

behind my red hot poker face
lies a fire near the warehouse space

...and the play's the thing...

[CURTAIN NUMBER ONE]

Out from the magic hat comes scapegoat Fish
the school mob swaging its flanks

against the benches and the dark dock planks...
Ari Arli Arlah
Sentiment at last, matchsticks
a monument of sympathy simpatico
the justice and the jury
put the eight ball in his pocket (something for the road to nowhere)

With a smile.
    a glass of water ... sleep Sissy Fish   (Sisyphus)
        sleep with the fishes
        I have heard the mermaids singing each to each
        I don't think they will sing for me.

...And sure honesty pays off
in two cent increments
stolen wills and testaments.
Even Ozymandias had a monument...
                Head in the dirt.

in the rooms women come and go
writing of Ui in Cicero
ain't got no roots, ain't got no fruits
    But a flower
               ... Ui loves me. Ui loves me not."
But the smell ... oh-Roma
no salt can clean my nose this season.
             Ring around the rosie
             Pockets full of posies
             Ashes, ashes...
...Here, here will I show you fear,
        on the ball.
GET'M UP AGAINST THE WALL!
    heads, shoulders, knees, and toes...
I hear the pitter patter of Feet, Dull
            in the rooms women come and go
            writing of Ui in Cicero
            ('til human voices wake us and we drown)

[THE ETERNAL FOOTMAN?]

... and songs from a farther room
                    "UP AGAINST THE WALL!!!"
head, shoulders, knees, and toes,
knees and toes,
knees and toes,
heads, shoulders, knees, and toes,
kiss your arse goodbye...
"Friends, Roma's, countrymen,
   lend me your years   (1984)
   lend me your rears   (ONE GIANT BOOT IS STAMPING)
   lend me your ears:

Step right up
cast your votes
your choice is free
(death costs nothing)

"this is the way the world ends"
"this is the way the world ends"
"this is the way the world ends"
"not with a bang"   (We are the hollow men)

but a whimper

Shantih, Shantih, Shantih.

15 Problems of Performance Analysis

The aims and purposes of performance analysis within the curriculum of theatre studies are focused on one aspect: how is it possible to accord to the desired competences particular practices which can be trained?

    To determine the elements that should form such a course one has to be aware of the following problems:

    1. Prerequisites of a performance analysis

- How is it possible that I analyze a process which is ephemeral and transitory?
- Problems of documentation, notation, description.
- How to perceive as well as to describe theatrical events?

2. Object of analysis or What is to be analyzed?

- What happens on stage?
- What happens between stage and auditorium?
- What happens during the rehearsals?
- What happens in the individual spectator?

3. Devices of analysis

- How to describe what one perceives?
- Why do we need a particular terminology for this purpose?
- How to develop particular questions to be dealt with in the analysis?
- Problems of constituting meaning.
- Position and function of the performance in different contexts.
- Consideration of a general (or particular) knowledge in theatre and cultural history.

4. Relationship between theory and praxis

- How far is it desirable to focus on the "object"?
- Is it effective to refer to particular theories explicitly?
- Which kind of theories are suitable for this purpose?

As headline for the kind of qualifications and competences the students are supposed to acquire, I have chosen "Thinking capable of intervention", the known basic attitude of Brecht to discover essentials of the dramaturgy and the impact of a production we discussed.[1] Here **Brandon Sch's** observations:

---

[1] *The Resistible Rise of Arturo Ui* by Bertolt Brecht, PTTP, University of Delaware, Hartshorn Theatre, Newark, opening performance March 11, 1999 with Carine Montbertrand as Arturo Ui.

"Let me begin by saying that seeing the production of *The Resistible Rise of Arturo Ui* has created many more questions than it has answered. As a student of Brecht over the past two months, my main endeavors have been to grasp a notion of Brecht's theories, ideas, philosophies of the "epic theatre", etc. Whether subject to the format of my lecture, or to a lack on my part for fuller research, I was not in the least bit aware of the technique or flavor with which a Brecht show is produced. While my research and my eyes have witnessed seemingly different aspects of Brecht, their junction meets at the fact that I had a lot of fun.

"What did seeing *Ui!* remind me of? Vaudeville ... a dingy cabaret, the plague, Albrecht Dürer, Scarface, the Tracy Ullman Show, the paintings of Francis Bacon ... the cinematography of Oliver Stone, and many other mixed media images floated through my head during the show (and currently as I remember it). It was not what I envisioned at all when reading or studying Brecht. To watch Brecht thought, would be an intellectual stretch or leap, requiring a bit of effort on the audience member. Although now it seems a naïve assumption about the 'epic theatre', I also thought Brecht's productions would be relatively simple. Needless to say that assumption is dispelled. The complicated technical work put into *Ui!* must have been a nightmare; let alone to teach the ensemble their parts. Taking technology into consideration, certainly Brecht's contemporary audiences must have been watching a loud, pulsating, half-mechanical, half-organic beast of a show.

"God, it was fun. What was it that amazingly astounded every age group in the audience that afternoon? An old woman in front of me could hardly control her little old granny-fanny joy at witnessing such a spectacular event. And this was a show filled with bawdy movement, explicit language and violence, and whose theme mirrored an all too familiar story of genocide and conquest. Not for grannies. Brecht apparently knew that these things appealed to all people, but in what way? Perhaps it was his use of 'Verfremdung', the alienation effects employed to distance the audience from getting personally involved in the drama.

"The audience was watching the word 'fuck' used; it wasn't being screamed at them for once ... You only have to watch the news to see who died today.

"Concerning the 'Verfremdung', I was surprised this theory was splattered over everything in the show. I assumed it would be used sparingly, and thus creating a greater effect of distancing faster. But it seems no stone was left unturned. The propaganda handed out, the white faces, the enormous platform with air brakes, the scene transitions (!), the white rubber-like walls, the upstage wall with large slits allowing us to see the offstage actors, and virtually everything else was truly what my friends and I call 'whacked out'. It was just crazy.

"This all-encompassing attention to the detail of alienating the audience did almost the opposite to me. I found myself drawn into analyzing and scrutinizing the detail of transitions and the skill in scene manipulation. The actress playing Arturo Ui was a magnet for my eyes; I strained to follow all of her strange quirks and facial contortions.

"Is this what Brecht is trying to avoid? You could truly lose yourself in Ui's walk of dementia and the twisted smiles of Giri and Givola. Was it because I was familiar with the story? I don't think so. I think it was because I had never seen anything like that before in my life.

"I like theatre. I want to make theatre. Is this paradox the reason why Brecht has failed to transform the theatre into an art for the modern human? For certainly, the theatre today is still mainly of the Aristotelian crew, found on the principles of Shakespeare. To be an actor, the height of my learning could possibly be found in none other than the Royal Shakespeare Company ... if all I needed was a job. Brecht may have wowed and thrilled his audiences, but was there anything changed in their minds? Is Brechtian theatre a catalyst for changing the role of theatre, or is his form a future standard for when that task has already been accomplished? I don't know why all new plays aren't like the ones of *Ui!* I saw. We like them.

"I suppose the history surrounding Brecht's own rise is irrelevant in considering the theatre of today and what it will do. The fact remains that I, along with everyone else in the audience that afternoon had their minds blown. It was more than a play to watch, it was something to take from and keep. *Ui!* gave me a taste of just how 'epic' the theatre can be.

"And I mean like *Led Zeppelin* epic. Big humongous planets hitting each other ... Krypton exploding ... clown school ... the nuns hitting you."

The description of the performance is an example for the ability to analyze structured complexes. The way of observing gives insights into the problems of meaning attribution and "use value" of the performance. The discussion in the seminar about the theatrical event soon focused on the incomplete nature of the play-script. The fact that the allocation of various non-verbal elements to pre-existing words determines the specific nature of the dialogue of the performance-text, supports the thesis that these elements reflect more than anything else the intentions and purposes of the director.

16 On Experimental Theatre*

The aim and object of all theatre work is to make the story lucid, always to find the most topical reading of the plays and to communicate it from the stage. We must not consider a certain form, a definite structure to be the only theatrically correct one, to be alone important or necessary. Such a dogmatic approach would severely limit the possibilities of theatre. On the other hand, one cannot just simply interchange forms of presentation and communication at will. Theatre is more than a mediation of ideas, or rationally graspable content. Theatre is mediated via the senses, and is thus basically a sensual phenomenon. It is the total theatre that people respond to – the information or content plus the way in which this is presented to the senses. Thus, how theatre is produced, how one communicates, can never be a matter of indifference. Theatre that works with grotesque, fantastic artistry and metaphoric abstractions must have a different effect than theatre which – to name its opposite – conjures up exact illusionary pictures in real relations of time and space via the language and the fourth wall convention.

A theatre that realizes itself through fantastic exaggerations, metaphors, artistic abstraction and seeks to communicate with the spectators about reality in this way can have a strong stimulating effect on the imagination and thus activate an audience's general behavior. Such an enjoyable, productive exertion of the imagination is also stamped by the new, strange, unfamiliar images which are conjured up through artistically exaggerating social relations, individual attitudes and social/historical processes. Unrealistic theatre which aims at progressive, democratic and revolutionary involvement in reality (and it is this type of theatre we are mainly concerned with here) the point is to mentally reduce such fantastic forms and images which belong exclusively to the theatre to their significance for reality, i.e., for social and individual behavior. This demands greater effort from the imagination; it actually stimulates the imagination. And it exactly is that I consider to be an important function for historically progressive art ...

---

*First published in [17].

III Training Exercises

"Now, tell me ... give me one word, a verb, which will intensify your line of action."
"To please the Governor."
*"To **win** his heart... This is your task to obtain an invitation. Well, sir, how will you act?"*

(Konstantin Stanislavsky, quoted in [55, p. 44])

17 Creating Situations

In the act of discovering verbs "with which to label the characters dominant preoccupations at given points in a play, the actors also supply themselves with reasons for doing what their characters do", described once a student at the Malmö Theatre Academy[1] his rehearsal experience with non-Stanislavskian vocabulary. Whatever aesthetic roots the participants had, all agreed, above all, to develop the scheme of the character's physical behavior in each episode and to unite them later in a single line of action. The practical problem is, that the actor's reasons for performing a certain action are identical with those of the character he creates. That fact helps to generate the impression that the character and the actor are one.

Perform the following scenes (quoted from conventional material for "improvisations") using one of the suggested cliche situations. Before the performance take 2–3 minutes time to read the text and find a strong, "surprising" contradiction in the story you plan to narrate.

Scene: What did you do last night?

---

[1]During the academic year 2003/2004 I had been invited by the Swedish Academy of Arts to participate in the establishment of a Directing Department at the Malmö Theatre Academy/University of Lund. During this assignment I also had the opportunity to teach a workshop "Acting and Dramaturgy", using scenes of plays by Brecht and Shakespeare as well as non-sense prose.

A: Hi!
B: Hello.
A: How's everything?
B: Fine. I guess.
A: Do you know what time it is?
B: No. Not exactly.
A: Don't you have a watch?
B: Not on me.
A: Well?
B: Well what?
A: What did you do last night?
B: What do you mean?
A: What did you do last night?
B: Nothing.
A: Nothing?
B: I said, nothing!
A: I'm sorry I asked.
B: That's all right.

Situations:

1. 'A' is a parent; 'B' is a teenager. The scene takes place at the breakfast table; 'B' eating a bowl of cereal, 'A' entering.

2. 'A' and 'B' (different sexes) are a young married couple. Last night, after an argument, 'B' left the apartment. It is now the following morning. 'A' is washing dishes. 'B' returns.

3. 'A' and 'B' (same sex) are roommates. Both have been involved with the same boy (or girl) during the past few weeks, both are still interested in pursuing the relationship, both are somewhat suspicious of the other's secrecy. They meet while returning to their room after a night's absence.

4. 'A' and 'B' (same sex) are auditioning for an important role. It is rumored that the director plays sexual favorites in casting. 'A' and 'B' meet at the bulletin board to await the announcement of call-backs.

5. 'A' and 'B' are siblings. 'B' has recently been released from jail. After 'B' has stayed out all night, 'A' discovers him drunk in a park.

When many variations on content-less scenes are performed, with the actors switching partners each time, several things become evident: The content of the scene is created entirely by the given situation and the actors: The words become instruments of the action, not the dictator of plot, character, or behavior. Thus the acting becomes a way of creating a spontaneously changing relationship – and the plot develops entirely out of what happens between you and your acting partner.

With the following scene focus on different audiences and environments. Experience how your performance changes, if you address a specific story. A wide range of circumstances – from presenting the scene at a youth camp, on Broadway or in an elderly home – will challenge you to focus on appropriately representative physical elements. Use the same situations as before.

Scene: I'm going away.

A: Hi!
B: Hello.
A: You all right?
B: Yes.
A: Are you sure?
B: Yes, I'm sure. A little headache, that's all.
A: Oh good. You want some aspirin?
B: No. Don't be so helpful, OK?
A: You are upset.
B: Good Lord!
A: Ok, OK. I thought you might want to talk.
B: About what?
A: About anything.
B: I'm going away.
A: What do you mean?
B: I'm going away, that's all.
A: Where?
B: Not far. Don't get excited.
A: When?

B: Now. (STARTS TO LEAVE.)

The training should be conducted in such stages, that one can experience an escalation from the passing of personal barriers to overcoming more objective conceptions and to the limits of ability. Acting exercises in the context of performance study is a dramaturgical tool to develop a "distanced" perspective for the scenic events. A young actress, who worked on the change of attitudes of Mother Courage in the scene "The Great Capitulation" during the Malmö workshop summarized the new relationship to the audience she had experienced: "You have to care passionately about the *point* of the demonstration without becoming unduly caught up in the demonstration *itself*."

18 Physical Expression

There is no doubt, that the ability to make a selected situation visible on stage needs physical awareness. Starting with copying other people's behavior through demonstrating it, our body becomes by nature narrative. That is a most basic and essential experience. Exercises for a training of such "self-revelation" can be found in the training repertoire of Rudolf Laban, Etienne Decrous, Gret Palucca, Jacques Lecoq, Mary Wigmann or Vsevolod Meyerhold. Working with choreographers like Andrew Tsubaki, Eva Winkler and Patrico Bunster to condition ensembles for professional performances of classical plays taught me the cross-overs and intersections of physical theatre. In recent year I focus on the foregrounding of the body and the origins of theatre in both play and human cognition.

In *Towards a Poor Theatre* by Jerzy Grotowski, there is an exercise [13, p. 147] called 'flight', which clearly extends the limits of a purely personal conception of ability:

1. Squatting on the heels... hop and sway like a bird ready to take flight...

2. Still hopping, raise yourself into an upright position, while the hands flap like wings...

3. Take off in flight with successive forward movements...

4. Land like a bird.

The example shows, that the actor must strive to make viable the impossible.

Acrobatics liberate the actor from the laws of gravity – at least as we know from *Theatre Laboratory*, *Complicite* or *Theatre du Soleil* to an extent never before deemed possible.

Expression through movement and physicality examines the physiological relationship between bodily action and emotional experience. It improves the understanding of the acting process and is a must for any introduction to performance.

To turn from Grotowski's demands to a complete different imagination, I like to quote Marcel Marceau, the mime. He gave interviews frequently, sometimes in the character Bip's clothes, explaining him to the crowd: "If I do this, I feel that I am a bird. If I do this, I am a fish. And I feel that, if I do this, it's like a song... To mime the wind, one becomes a tempest. Mime expresses... the soul's most secret aspiration." [41] The beauty of physical action always remains close to the ground – it takes its pictures out of the emotional memory of the people, the spectators observing the performance.

19 Storytelling

Performance is not merely a representation of real-life behavior, but a demonstration which can reveal new truth about that behavior. While the actor, for example, is singing the popular melody of "Mack the Knife", we realize that the lyrics are in fact blood-curdling, so that the tension between form and content forces us to a shocking realization of Brecht's point of view.

Acting exercises are the search for *gest* or *gestus* of the action:

- Who is the sentence of use to?

- Who does it claim to be of use to?

- What does it call for?

- What practical action corresponds to it?

- What sort of sentences result from it?

- What sort of sentences support it?

• In what situation it is spoken? By whom?

The purpose, then, is to perform selected but recognizable details of human behavior in a manner and context, which causes them to seem suddenly unfamiliar and revealing, permitting the audience to perceive and judge them more clearly.

The following two "non-dramatic" texts use narrative devices similar to those which Aristotle described for the *epic* poem:

Excerpt From a Speech of Pericles[2]

Our constitution does not copy the laws of neighboring states; we are rather a pattern to others than imitators ourselves. Its administration favors the many instead of the few; this is why it is called a democracy. If we look to the laws, they afford equal justice to all in their private differences; if to social standing, advancement in public life falls to reputation for capacity, class considerations nor being allowed to interfere with merit; nor again does poverty bar the way ... Nor are these the only points in which our city is worthy of admiration. We cultivate refinement without extravagance and knowledge without effeminacy; wealth we employ more for use than for show, and place the real disgrace of poverty not in owning to the fact but in declining to struggle against it. Our public men have, besides politics, their private affairs to attend to, and our ordinary citizens, though occupied with the pursuits of industry, are still fair judges of public matters; for, unlike any other nation, regarding him who takes no part in these duties not as unambitious but as useless, we Athenians are able to judge at all events if we cannot originate, and instead of looking on discussion as a stumbling block in the way of action, we think it an indispensable preliminary to a wise action ... In short, I say that as a city we are the school of Hellas.

A Poem by Cesar Vallejo: Have you anything to say in your defense?

Well, on the day I was born,

---

[2] quoted by Thucydides, *History of the Peloponnesian War* [54].

God was sick.
They all know that I'm alive,
That I'm vicious; and they don't know
the December that follows from that January
Well, on the day I was born,
God was sick.

There is an empty place
in my metaphysical shape
that no one can reach:
a cloister of silence
that spoke with the fire of its voice muffled.

On the day I was born,
God was sick.

Brother, listen to me, Listen...
oh, all right. Don't work, I won't leave
without taking my Decembers along,
without leaving my Januaries behind.
Well, on the day I was born,
God was sick.
They all know that I'm alive,
that I chew my food... any they don't know
why harsh winds whistle in my poems,
the narrow uneasiness of a coffin,
winds untangles from the Sphinx
who holds the desert for routine questioning.

Yes they all know... Well, they don't know
that the light gets skinny
and the darkness gets bloated...
And they don't know that the Mystery joins things
together...
that he is a hunchback
musical and sad who stands a little way off
and foretells
the dazzling progression from the limits to

the Limits.
On the day I was born,
God was sick,
gravely.

20 Physical Punctuation

The following exercise trains how a change in a physical rhythm coordinates with a change in the plot or in a character's intention or understanding of a relationship.

Select any speech that you have memorized, possibly one from the previous exercise, and deliver it to a (real or imaginary) partner while doing a repetitive physical action, such as:

1. Jogging in place

2. Skipping rope

3. Beating egg yolks

4. Doing sit-ups

5. Combing your hair

6. Playing the piano

7. Dribbling a (pretend) basketball

8. Shaving

Talk "over" the physical action; make yourself understood – and your intentions felt – be aware of the distraction of your movement.

Now "punctuate" the speech by stopping your movement at a certain point in the text. Experiment with several possible moments. Experiment with stopping one movement – and later in the speech starting another one. It is a first step to create different actions with the same text and to experience your own physical presence as the base for performing the dramatists text in visible situations.

IV Analyzing Plays

*The theatre is a search for an expression
that is directly concerned with the quality of living.*

(Peter Brook, in A.C.H. Smith, Orghast at Persopolis [51, p. 1])

21 The Plough and the Stars by Sean O'Casey – A Study Outline

Background   Background – Concept to be developed:

Sean O'Casey came out of nowhere in the early 1920's to have several plays produced by the Abbey Theater in Dublin, Ireland. Among them, three have been considered to have been his finest:

> *The Shadow of a Gunman*
> *Juno and the Paycock*
> *The Plough and the Stars*

They were vitally Irish, tightly dramatic and frequently comic in their projection of Dublin experience as the time of "the troubles". One group of Dubliners reacted violently against the third of those plays in 1926 and there were disturbances in the theater.

"The troubles" refers to the years 1916 to 1923 which were years of terror and violence. From the outbreak of the Easter Week Rebellion in 1916 to the final victory of the Free State Government over the rebels in 1923, no peace of mind or safety of person was possible for the mass of Irish – Protestant or Catholic, Nationalist or Republican, worker or employer. The struggle for Irish independence, carried on for hundreds of years, was reaching its climax. As in other struggles for independence, various leaders and movements, each claiming to be the voice and the way, issued manifestoes, armed their followers and broke the heads of those who disagreed with them. Disillusion, blind hatred and confusion, as well as idealism and heroism, were expressed in the speeches and actions of the innumerable factions participating in the struggle. In the name of freedom and liberty, Irish fought British, free Stater fought Ulsterman, Protestant fought Catholic and Sinn Fein fought Sinn Fein. Organized armies, bands of gunmen and individual assassins roamed the land. The order of the day was curfews, military zones, martial law, executions, looting and expropriation of land and property. Yet, through it all shone the high ideas of Wolfe Tone, Robert Emmet and Charles Parnell; through it all the magic word freedom inspired a nation that had suffered and sacrificed. Here were people, after years of strife, on the threshold of destiny – the dams of common sense, restraint, tolerance were not strong enough to check the flood-tides of frenzied patriotism, unbridled excesses and intolerance.

It is in this setting that the three plays of Sean O'Casey's Irish national period are laid.

Synopsis   The setting is in the Dublin slums during the Easter Week Rebellion of 1916. At this time, the defense arm of the labor movement (the Citizen Army) and the Sinn Fein military organization (the Irish Volunteers), after going their separate ways for some time, united their forces to challenge the rule of Britain.

The first act opens in November, 1915, and we are introduced to the various inhabitants of a tenement. Nora Clitheroe, a young sensitive wife; Jack Clitheroe, her husband, and officer in the Citizen Army; the Young Covey, cousin to Jack and a Socialist, Peter Flynn, uncle to Nora, an excitable, fussy man: Fluther Good, a loud-mouthier, hard-drinking carpenter; Bessie Burgess, loyalist, whose son is fighting with the British in France; Mrs. Gogan, a charwoman; and Mollser, her daughter, a consumptive.

The second act takes place in a public house, outside of which a meeting is being held by the leaders of the independence movement. The words of the speaker (alleged to be the actual words from the address which Padraig Pearse proclaimed the Republic) drift into the pub.

In the pub, Rosie, a prostitute, is complaining about the lack of business since the men are meeting and "thinking of higher things than a girls' garters" sic. The Young Covey, filled with self-importance and socialist doctrines, sneers at the kind of freedom, national liberation, proclaimed by the speaker.

Bessie Burgess, loyalist that she is, complains that she cannot understand how the Irish "… Can call themselves Catholics, when they won't lift a finger to help poor little Catholic Belgium." She is threatened by Gogan. The two women soon drop politics and switch to slandering each other's virtue; Rosie's honor is defended by Fluther when the Young Covey calls her a prostitute; Rosie rewards Fluther by accepting his invitation for a few drinks before he sees her home. The plough and the stars are forgotten when there is drinking, fighting, and quibbling to be done. Even at the end of the act, when Captain Brennar, Lieutenant Langon and Commander Clitheroe respectively cry: "Imprisonment for the Independence of Ireland", "Wounds for the Independence of Ireland" and "Death for the Independence of Ireland"; their defiant utterances become lost as Rosie, hanging on the arm of Fluther, sings a song.

The third act takes place during the Easter Week Rebellion. Nora, in a frenzy over the safety of her husband has searched the bullet-riddled streets for him in vain and is finally brought back to the tenement by Fluther. Later, Jack does appear but is deaf to the pleas of Nora to desert the struggle. He leaves her to rejoin his comrades.

However, for the inhabitants of the tenement, the revolution, the ailing Mollser, political differences and even personal danger are forgotten when the word gets around that there is looting going on nearby. Another army marches off, but this time with baby carriages and hand carts to bring home the spoils of non-participation. The Act closes with Bessie Burgess heroically volunteering to go through the streets of Dublin to fetch a doctor for the completely distraught Nora.

The fourth act brings the play to a swift and tragic conclusion. Nora loses her mind, Jack Clitheroe is killed in action, Mollser dies of consumption and Bessie Burgess is mortally wounded by the Tommies. Fluther and the Young Covey are taken into custody by the British as in the distance we hear the booming of artillery, the rattle of machine gun fire and the singing of a patriotic song by the rebels and "Keep the Home Fires Burning" by the British.

Vocabulary Development

Dublin city and county borough and part of the Republic of Ireland. It is situated at the mouth of the Liffey River on Dublin Bay.

Wolfe Tone, Robert Emmet and Charles Parnell Irish revolutionists of the 18th, 19th and 20th centuries.

Sinn Fein a society for the furtherance of all things Irish which in 1910 split into two groups. The older version was unsympathetic toward labor, frowned on strikes and alienated those Nationalist who's first loyalty was to the working classes of the world rather than to all classes of the Irish nation. The new Sinn Fein preached against sweated labor, supported strikers and the labor movement. It was essentially Socialist.

The Plough and the Stars the symbol on the flag of the Citizen Army. The stars represent the ideal, the plough and the reality.

Tragedy a serious drama typically describing a conflict between the protagonist and a superior force (as destiny) and having a sorrowful or disastrous conclusion that excites pity or terror.

Bibliography

Koslow, Jules. *The Green and the Red: Sean O'Casey, the man and his plays*. Art Inc, New York, 1950.

Malone, Maureen and Moore, Harry T. *The Plays of Sean O'Casey: Crosscurrents/Modern Critiques*. Southern Illinois University Press, 1969.

O'Casey, Sean. *The Man and his Plays*. Golden Griffin Books, New York, 1949.

———. *Selected Plays*. Macmillan, New York, 1954.

Questions

1. Sean O'Casey calls *The Plough and the Stars* a tragedy. How does this play differ from the classical concepts of tragedy?

2. What are some other examples of modern tragedy? What is it that makes them so? How do they depart from the Greek or Shakespearean idea? Two examples are Theodore Dreiser's *An American Tragedy* (novel) and Arthur Miller's *Death of a Salesman* (play).

3. What has O'Casey in common with Yeats, Synge and Beckett?

22 Summarizing Actions and Events (King Oedipus) *

The legend of Oedipus is as follows: King Laois of Thebes and his wife Jocasta were told in Delphi (by the God Apollo) that their son would kill his father and marry his mother. To avoid this calamity, the parents hand their newborn son, whose feet are pierced and bound together, to a shepherd, who has been ordered to leave the infant on a hillside to die of exposure. But he hands him over to a Corinthian shepherd, who takes him to the King of Corinth. So the boy, called "swollen foot" (Oedipus) because of his crippled feet, is brought up at the Corinthian court, regarding King Polybos and Queen Merope as his parents.

Troubled about allusions from his playmates, the young man goes to Delphi to find out the truth about his descent, only to be told by the oracle that he would kill his father and marry his mother. In order to avoid this, young Oedipus does not return to Corinth but travels towards Thebes. On his way he meets a stranger whom he slays after a quarrel, not knowing that it is none other than his father. Not far from Thebes a sphinx bars his way into the town. As Oedipus is able to solve her puzzle, he is allowed to continue his travel. By solving the puzzle, he has also freed the town from the burden of this monster. In recognition of his deed, he is put on the throne of Thebes getting as his wife, Queen Jocasta, his mother. For many years he reigns for the benefit of the town and the obliviously happy couple has four children: two sons, Polyneices and Eteokles, and two daughters, Ismene and Antigone.

The drama *King Oedipus* begins while the plague is raging in Thebes: Oedipus has sent his brother-in-law Creon for advice to Delphi. When he learns that murder is brooding over the town, and King Laois' murderer must be found and punished, Oedipus tries to throw light upon the crime, in order to save the town from epidemic. Even as it dawns upon him that he himself may be the person wanted, he continues the investigation until he knows the truth. Oedipus himself executes the punishment intended for the murderer: blinding himself and leaving the town as an outcast. Full of distress and shame Jocasta hangs herself.

Now Jocasta's brother, Creon, comes into play as the prospective ruler of Thebes. He rules as regent until Polyneices and Eteocles come of age. Oedipus also entrusts

---

*Excerpt from the dramaturgical material of a production of *King Oedipus* by Euripides with the Theatre Department of Villanova University. The opening performance took place on December 4, 1994, at the Vasey Theatre.

him with the guardianship over the two girls Antigone and Ismene.

The story continues with Oedipus at Colonnus, which presents up to the final coronation of Creon in Thebes. Oedipus driven by great unrest, wandering the countryside, accompanied and cared for by his daughter, Antigone. At Colonnus he finds the death he longed for. Meanwhile back in Thebes, the grown-up sons of Oedipus, Polyneices and Eteocles, have wrested the throne from Creon and fight amongst themselves for sole possession of it. Eteocles, the elder brother, finally banishes his brother and claims the throne.

In Argos the refugee, Polyneices, finds support for his cause. With an Argive army, he lays siege to Thebes to claim his throne. At this point, Antigone, informs by Ismene about the impending brothers' battle, hurriedly returns to Thebes with her to prevent immanent fratricide. However, they are not successful and the brothers are both killed by each others hands. The play *Antigone* begins with the aftermath of this battle.

23 The Legend (Antigone)

The drama *Antigone* is part of the Oedipus story. Based on traditional heroic legends Sophocles created a new version for the Athenians of the 5th century B.C. in his three tragedies *King Oedipus*, *Oedipus in Colonos* and *Antigone*. Although *Antigone* was written first (442 B.C., followed by *King Oedipus* 15 years later and *Oedipus in Colonos* 35 years later), it looks as if it were written immediately after the other two plays. But it constitutes only the final part of the story about the Oedipus family and is one of his earlier plays.

The legend of Oedipus is as follows:

King Laios of Thebes and his wife Jocasta were told in Delphi (by the god Apollo) that their son would kill his father and marry his mother. To avoid this calamity the parents hand their new-born son, whose feet are pierced and bound together, to a shepherd, who has been ordered to leave the infant on a hillside to die of exposure. But he hands him over to a Corinthian shepherd, who takes him to the king of Corinth. So the boy, called "swollen foot" (Oedipus) because of his crippled feet, is brought up at the Corinthian court, regarding King Polybos and Queen Merope as his parents.

Troubled about allusions from his playmates, the young man goes to Delphi to find out the truth about his descent, only to be told by the oracle that he would kill his father and marry his mother. In order to avoid this, young Oedipus does not return to Corinth but travels towards Thebes. On his way he meets a stranger whom he slays after a quarrel, not knowing that it is none other than King Laios himself, his father. Not far from Thebes a sphinx bars his way into town. As Oedipus is able to solve her puzzle, he is allowed to continue his travel. By solving the puzzle he has also freed the town from the burden of this monster. In recognition of his deed he is put on the throne in Thebes, getting as his wife Queen Jocasta, his mother. For many years he reigns for the benefit of the town, and the obliviously happy couple has for children: two sons, Polyneices and Eteocles, and two daughters, Ismene and Antigone.

The drama *King Oedipus* begins while the plague is raging in Thebes: Oedipus has sent his brother-in-law Creon for advice to Delphi. When he learns that murder is brooding over the town, and king Laios' murderer must be found and punished, Oedipus tries to throw light upon the crime, in order to save the town from the epidemic. Even as it dawns upon him that hew himself may be the person wanted he continues the investigation until he knows the truth.

Oedipus himself executes the punishment intended for the murderer: blinding himself and leaving the town as an outcast. Full of distress and shame Jocasta hangs herself.

Now Jocasta's brother Creon comes into play as the perspective ruler of Thebes. He rules as regent until Polyneices and Eteocles come of age. Oedipus also entrusts him with the guardianship over the tow girls Antigone and Ismene.

24 Processes are Narrated as Changeable (Hekabe)*

Putting *Hekabe* on stage would require a proliferation of the Euripides' views on theatre. It would mean a proliferation of all the contradictions, absurdities, apparent rudiments and contrasts in a myth-covered tradition. They have a topical function, as the thesis says, for Euripides. Admittedly, this is also no restriction; they are part and parcel of an elaborate reciprocal fabric of relationships which

---

*Excerpt from the conceptional material for the 1983 production of DESMI on the occasion of the Athens Festival / First Cultural Capital of Europe. The opening performance took place on August 16, 1983, with Aspassia Papathanassiou as Hecuba.

must have functioned within an overall structure that can only be anticipated by us. It is only in the performance that the driving motivations and relations of his figures and events enclosed in the text are made to a preemptive stimulus of his own living relationships within its original function, to the play itself. The "strategy of action" lies in the way of narration itself, namely, how individual events, historical state actions and contemporary experiences are coupled with each other. This strategy encourages the public to contemplate its responsibility in the clashes of the time. This strategy implies kind of learning process, permeating the temporal, dramatic and psychological fabric. Euripides teaches us to enjoy the ability for the self-determination of the social line of development. *Hekabe* is such a field of experimentation for human self-responsibility.

Hekabe calls for gestic theatre performance. The behavior of the figures has to be explicably derived from the situations. The events appear to be strikingly historical; the action itself reveals, at the same time, the memorizing coupling back to the ancient myths and the controversial emergence of a new historical awareness, with testimony adduced on the process of origin.

Against the backdrop of the seemingly unusual conflicts happening on a remote "Level of Kings" one needs to discover the palpable contradictions of concrete men having identifiable interests and class connections. The question is how does Euripides seek new values and norms from the conditions of human living together: how to evolve new values from reason and from earthly responsibility?

When we assume that a destiny originally conceived of as sensible and sacred is now appearing rather as a blindly furious accident vis-à-vis the self-posed independent man, the theatre of Euripides should have developed into a place where the citizen of Athena was able to recognize his emotions, his ideas and his social position. What could be heard and watched on the stage there, was no longer a sequence of events proceeding with the coercive consistency of natural events, but rather a way of acting that was probably out to bring about attitudes in the audience, definite approaches, and the border situations of complex characters were bound to perceive slight discrepancies in society.

The facts worth seeing are that there is a tangible quality of contradiction in the behavior of "history-making persons". The process of decision-making for *Hekabe*, for instance, raises questions of strategy and tactics in political processes, the revaluation of conventions, also correlations of ideology and morale and the discovery of women's emotional life. (...) It has to be made obvious how Euripides portrays the contradicting motivations, how he unravels semblance and essence, and how he asserts the idiosyncrasies of human behavior.

In *Hekabe* the step from the gesture of the tragedy, the still mystic trance, to the way of mediation, the already-theatrical function of language, has already been made. Language is no longer rhetoric, but already process, social relation. For this reason the gestic aspect has to be determined in the process of search, in the decision for this and for no other formulation. The meditative performance is not allowed to blur out anything. What is most amazing with the events is the contradiction between the statement of the text and the behavior of the figures. (...) Actors, instead of rhapsodists, provide a socially exactly determined fantasy filled design of reality which is inextricably linked, or will have to be linked with the virtual 'acting-out' of our possibilities of imaging the world. The questions of war and peace and those of power and justice, the hopes for historical and human changeability require distance and proximity: inconceivable and inexhaustible. Peremptorily, Euripides calls upon these responsible to be held accountable for peace and war ... and this is no longer a divine trick.

25 Basic Attitudes (The Good Person of Szechwan)*

The aims of Brecht's theatre were clear from the first performances; a depiction of the social relations affecting human beings in a clear and precise but also aesthetically pleasing and exciting manner for the audience to judge themselves and amend where necessary.

The story of Shen Te is known as the golden fable where three gods come to earth. They are looking for a good person whose behavior justifies their teachings and the present state of the world. They receive the hospitality of the prostitute Shen Te, the poorest of poor. The gods reward her with 1000 silver dollars and they command her: "To be good with others, as well as, with yourself."

With the gift of the gods Shen Te is in a position to buy a small tobacco shop. Now she can satisfy her desire to be good with everyone. She is kind to all those in need, giving like the goddess of the horn of Amalthia. So Shen Te finds herself

---

*Excerpt from the dramaturgical material for the 1977 production of the National Theatre of Cyprus (THOC) at the Municipal Theatre of Nicosia. The opening performance took place on October 13, 1977, with Despina Bebedeli as Shen Te/Shui Ta.

quickly out on the streets. She takes the form of an imaginary cousin who is tough and rigid. She uses this trick three times. On the first occasion the cousin saves her tobacco shop; her friends as well as her exploiters gain from this. On the second occasion he helps her lover, the impoverished pilot Sun, by finding money for him so he can buy a position. The third time the cousin protects the baby that Shen Te is expecting.

She Te guards her baby like a tiger wanting to protect it from a miserable life. She tries to balance the qualities of Shen Te and Shui Ta but her cousin's way leads her to unsolvable conflicts. The "angel of the slums" becomes the "scourge of the slums." The gods' command cannot be achieved, even with tricks. Something is rotten in the state of Szechwan. Its structure does not allow to be good with others and with yourself...

To understand Brecht's message we concentrate on this: the adjustment to the situation or the effort to use it for one's own profit is at the same time disregarding human values.

Brecht shows the productivity of human beings, who are decaying in the case of Szechwan. In the people there are more possibilities than those they can actually realize. We should show why people are like that, what makes everyone productive, and in what way people are prevented from developing their productivity.

The strange milieu of the play becomes alive from the acceptance of the ability for change inherent in the social structure. Szechwan of the parable is not an existing, but an imaginary, contemporary suburb. It would be misleading for the play to show a certain race, nationality or fashion. The actual events must be the center of attention so that the fantasy of the spectator can envisage many places similar to Szechwan. Chinoisierie would not be sufficient...

Change as a great source of pleasure – from Brecht's viewpoint this also entails conflict, clashes, and striding out along different paths. Pleasure includes the joy of trying things out, the thrill of making a find, and the burden of failure. In the same way as it is not easy for man to "come into his own," a theatre must constantly regenerate its self-perception, keeping in mind the conflicts that are always involved in the search for new ways of doing things.

26 Director's Notes (The Resistible Rise of Arturo Ui)*

1   The present day relevance of this play lies in the fact that – through numerous means of theatrical persuasive power – it allows one to experience how "the Ui-type within the capitalistic context and the small mindedness in Ui" (Haugk) pose a latent danger for bourgeois democracy. Forty years after Nazism was crushed, historical awareness is disappearing in many areas, and the fascination with fascist alternatives and structures is on the rise. Deliberately or through carelessness, phenomena are being ripped out of their historical framework and discussed in a "value-free" context. *Der unaufhaltsame Aufstieg des Arturo Ui* – written by Brecht in Finland in the Spring of 1941, when he was fleeing the encroaching Hitler dictatorship in Europe and on his way to the US – was not and is not a play about German National Socialism. It makes sense neither as a *roman à clef* — Givola = Goebbels, Ragg = Strasser, Dogsborough = Hindenburg — nor as a "general outline" of fascism. In his *Arbeitsjournal* Brecht describes the points he wants to make as follows: "In *Ui* it was a matter of letting the historical events shine through continually, while at the same time imbuing the 'outer covering' (which actually serves to uncover) with a life of its own, i.e. It has to work—theoretically speaking—even beyond the level of personalities..." (1.4.1941). Justifiably Haugk concludes: "If the 'outer covering' ... is an 'uncovering,' then that which is to be demonstrated cannot be something which covers." Ui, then, "does not signify Hitler, but rather those features which have been borrowed from Hitler and combined with other material in the Ui-figure mean something more." Parable (model world) and historical background (parallels) are woven together: the audience is constantly reminded to something beyond that which is actually being portrayed on the stage.

2   Brecht demands that the story-line be told in such a way that "the perpetrators of major political crimes... are exposed, preferably to ridicule..." His instructions are clear:

- The play is "an attempt to explain Hitler's rise to the capitalistic world by setting it in a milieu with which they are familiar."

---

*Excerpt from the director's notes for the 1984 production of the Municipal Theatre of Calamata (Greece). The opening performance took place on October 26, 1984, with Adonis Katsaris as Arturo Ui. First published in [16].

- "Ui is a parable play, written with the intention of destroying the dangerous, yet all too common, respect for great killers."

- "Common sense dare not let itself be intimidated when confronted with historicity; what is valid for us on the small scale we have to put into effect on the large."

- "The circle is intentionally drawn tight: it is limited to the level of state, industrialists, *Junkers*, and petty bourgeois. That suffices to realize the purpose in mind. The play does not intend to provide a general, basic outline of the historical situation in the thirties."

- The projected texts should reinforce "the development of those aspects which are presented in excerpt or panoptic form."

In the prologue of the play itself reference is made to structures which provide various forms of mediation and reception: the gangster story, the authentic report, and a story comparable to Richard III. Each of these approaches – if taken alone – would lead to a wrong conclusion, if one where not to seek out that which specifically applies to the time and space of the very real public to which the play is being presented. Brecht cites and uses them because of their potential to evoke complementary perspectives, for Ui is expressly not Richard III. Often scenes which resemble classical constellations turn out to be distinctly different than those of Shakespeare or Goethe. In the dramaturgy, seemingly familiar courses of events are reshaped, a process which gradually provokes intellectual discernment. Thus the made-to-measure pinstripe better suits our contemporary Tiger Taoka — with his 10 billion annual turnover as boss of Jamagutsi Rubber in Osaka, which runs the dock-worker agency for the port city of Kobe — than it does Clark, who is actually not a gangster at all. (In a ZDF TV program in the FRG aired on an evening in late October, the Japanese Jakusa[1] presented themselves as honorable businessmen, each of whom was quite obviously missing half of his left little finger — an alienation effect that might well have stemmed from Brecht himself.) The Italian-American Mafia or images straight out of Hollywood B-films, striking and revealing because they are traditionally close to the public, most nearly approximate authenticity. In short, concentrations, truncations, and diversions

---

[1] Jakusa = gangster

to mechanisms constitute bases for these social experiences as well. Hitler moustaches and Nazi paraphernalia would only lessen the effect.

3   To what end does Brecht employ what he called the "double alienation of gangster plot and grand style" (28.3.1941), when he warns, in the previously cited remark, "too close a link between the two plots (*Ganster* and *Nazi* plots) — that is to say a form in which the gangster plot would merely symbolize the other one — would be intolerable because no one would then be looking incessantly for the 'meaning' of this or that feature, would be trying to find the model for every figure..."(1.4.1941) That which constitutes an alienation effect for the German audience does not necessarily evoke the same reaction elsewhere. This was the case with regard to the US in 1941, since it was with an eye to the American theater that the prospective emigrant wrote the play. He wrote it for "Gods [sic] own country," which in its particular ideology apostrophized fascism as alien and as a product of other nations; in Ui that ostensibly so un-American thing was represented as an American possibility. In Brecht's approach, it becomes obvious where the potential lies. For certainly little would be accomplished if we attempted a kind of historical farce forty years after the fall of the Third Reich. Fascism had and has many faces: Nazism was not the only one and not the last, as the history of this century demonstrates. Both before and since, the Greek people have had to suffer, to a more than sufficient degree, the stranglehold of other manifestations.

4   Why should Ui's rise be shown as stoppable? Stoppable by whom? It is quite clear that Ui does not remain simply an agent of the trust; rather, his dictatorship becomes something more than the dictatorship of the trust. Where the bourgeois-capitalist system is inconsistent, where it perpetrates its crimes under the protection of particular norms and forms, it damages them. The "grand style" which links the Nazi and gangster plots, represents the public *modus vivendi* of these entrepreneurs and their politicians. It stands for two things: for a depraved way of carrying out major or state undertakings, one which greatly impresses the petty bourgeoisie; and for the exemplary shaping of a social gesture: a model of demagogy. Haugk calls its function: "compromise between the claims of the people upon those who rule and the ruling interests themselves." Brecht destabilized the antithesis between gangsters and grand style: crime and idealizing are depicted as homologous. Evoking the "higher principles" of political morality, in order to

"put a proper face" on immoral striving for profit, is exposed as a shabby enterprise, but at the same time it is shown to be an effective weapon of the ruling classes.

5   The language is a montage of colloquial and elevated expression, of big-city jargon and language of Elizabethan dramas, of plastic, direct expression and worn out clichés. The crass gesticulation of carnival theater stands alongside high poetic standards. The juxtaposition of iambic pentameter upon the low social niveau serves as a measure of the significance its actions have for society as a whole. The language is visual. For this reason it was open for the use of shadow theater dolls, which — much like the plebian Kragiosis[2] tradition — lend it aesthetic and political weight. The Reichstag fire trial, with its little known facts, had to be shown blatantly, both in meaning and form, as an exemplary precedent, the pattern of bourgeois justice. Right from the beginning, the dolls which replace were figures are established as means; Ui will therefore remain present on the stage area long after we have forgotten the transformation of the announcer into the role of Ui. The dolls offer a balance of playfulness and basic gesture which keeps one from forgetting that all art and all inquiries serve a purpose: i.e. To contrast the finesse as well as the ghastliness of our abilities and our growing strength. The lightness and colorfulness of the play with the dolls — carried out by six actresses — stands in contrast to the historical stage composition: the compelling transformations which it makes possible, relegate the responsibility for this performance to the actors. The masks are the bridges to the dolls: transformation, prelude, and gestural investigation.

27 Iphigenia in Aulis or
Who is a free man, and who is a slave?*

Excerpt from an interview by Glyn Hughes

---

[2] Trans. Note: Karagös = Hanswurst in Turkish shadow-plays, cf. Wahrig

*The interview had been conducted June 17, 2005 by phone for *Cyprus Weekly*. It refers to the workshop-production of the play for the International Summer Institute of Ancient Greek Drama and Theatre, Paphos-Droushia, Cyprus, opening August 3, 2005, at the Roman Odeon in Ancient Paphos

Hughes: What are the challenges, discoveries of this very irregular play by Euripides?

Haus: Our experiences as directors have taught us, to keep in mind all irregularities, all things we wondered about at the first re-reading and may have found strange, unexpected, different in the play than we expected. Discovery is comparison.

Hughes: The play is a tragedy, **but** an unorthodox one due to its ending.

Haus: The several comedic passages, such as the arrival of Clytemnestra and her first encounter with Achilles may well be intended by Euripides. I am not with Kitto, the scholar, who collects all contradictions and non-standards to qualify the text as a "thoroughly second-rate play". I suggest always to look as long as possible to all irregularities in a text's dramaturgy as hints for theatricality. In my experience this is the most efficient way to find some social use value.

Hughes: The question of all scholars is: What did Euripides mean to say in writing the play as it is? Did he wish simply to entertain an audience with a good plot? or is some "tragic illumination" to be found there?

Haus: As theatre people we can be less abstract. For us the audience, the crowd, participating in the performance, had the "tragic illumination" in their mind too. Their view habits were socially determined. We witness conflicts that may have been regarded, in Jacob Burckhardt's word, as "an inner fever of this highly privileged national organism." The "tragic hero" is once again the Greek nation (cf. Menelaus' remark in 370), whose folly has been involved it in war.

The English translator Vellacott makes a good point: "But here it appears in the persons of three leaders, while its total strength is near at hand and both seen and heard by persons on the stage - in the shape of a superstitious, brutal, and mutinous rabble of men whom the leaders call their army, but whose slaves they know themselves to be." (450, 517, 1020, 1269-71, 1346ff)

Hughes: Agamemnon's behavior is repeatedly called insane, so is the whole impulse which has launched the expedition against Troy.

Haus: Yes, but ... Contradictions history teaches itself: Agamemnon complains to his daughter that he is the slave of Hellas, but three lines later, that the sacrifice is necessary because "Hellas must be free"; while behind the scenes, destroying everyone's freedom, is the brute army, itself slave to superstition and the lust for loot.

The audience in Ancient time had the con-text in mind in following the events on the orchestra.

For example: The character of the Old Man is not just a tool for the development of the plot, I do agree with all, who see him as the one single-hearted adult in the events, to show clearly at the outset the duplicity and cowardice of the "king of men". Again we witness in Agamemnon how power is man-made, that what one says is not what one does. One can observe: Politics as way of existence. From beginning to end words and actions are presented to be judged by an audience, occupied to survive their reality, and in doing so, changing it, to make the community more habitable.

Hughes: What about the chorus and its different function, if we compare to other Ancient plays?

Haus: Events and characters are not been judged by the chorus. The playwright insists, that grasping history on stage is not an ideological process, but all actions observed preserve an overriding solidarity beyond political factions and interests. To be able to do so, he trusted the audience knowledge of myth and history and their social visions.

More than in other dramatic texts of the time you can grasp the Greeks concept, how much all is about the study of perfection.

Take Achilles. Known in Athens since the *Iliad*, but what Euripides shows is the opposite of this image. Achilles' behavior must surely appear gauche to the audience; by Clytemnestra, unaware of this, sees only what she was expecting to see, the "son of the goddess". His character too is an example how event by event story-telling on stage functions. It is a training ground for the politikon zoon.

Hughes: Our understanding of the meaning and purpose of our lives is closely bound up with our understanding of what it means to be a person, that is, with our understanding of what it means to be a person, that is, with our concept of the self.

Haus: I have argued in all my work that it is time to re-examine this concept. One of the benefits of doing *Iphigenia in Aulis* can be to teach the students, that its characters are not our contemporaries, but their chorus is. If we want to understand our ideals of radical autonomy and individual self-perfection, and why these ideals are degenerated into the pathological narcissism that afflicts our society today, we need to study and to experience of the Ancient Greeks. Furthermore, it is this kind of workshop that can draw us out of our narcissism. By looking carefully at how a playwright like Euripides leads to discover another kind of self, the Ancient extensive self, with its ideal not of autonomy and radical freedom, but of harmony and unity with the whole world of being. The Greeks thus not only give us a better understanding of the modern self; they remind us, that our own culture, our own past, contains experiences and ideals which can help us to transcend this self and find other ways of experiencing our social existence. The story-telling is about community. But the ideal of community embodied in the classical city-state has never been surpassed. It is, moreover, a fundamental part of our own culture: only in the West can we find man defined, as Aristotle defined him, as politikon zoon, a "political animal", that is living being specifically characterized by his participation in the life of the polis.

The effort to discover within the heterogeneous skene those common denominators that characterize the social institution of "theatre" throughout the ages present an ongoing challenge.

And according to Aristotle — and we have to make all participants understand and agree — narrative of such kind is the soul of drama.

V Interwoven Contexts

Theatre rests upon a sense of responsibility to the human community. It is a form of permanent discourse among fellow men.

(Giorgio Strehler at the fortieth anniversary of the Avignon festival in 1987 (quoted in [39, p. 583]))

28 Experiment and Mass Appeal: Theatre of the Weimar Republic*

"Expressionism" and "political theatre" are terms which inseparable link the artistic revolution and the glory of the theatre during the Weimar era. "Experiment" and "mass appeal" became synonyms for the radical avant-garde reforms of theatre during the years 1919 to 1933 in Germany. Again and again since then, these traditions mobilized new impulses. We call to mind the general politicization of cultural life in the late 60s and early 70s, especially concerning working modes in the theatre (cooperative management, collective directing and the founding of professional "free groups") and the politically critical concepts for the staffing of classical plays. The revival of agit-prop theatre forms from the 20s for modern "street theatre" and the acceptance of non-European forms, such as Augusto Boal's political theatre of the oppressed, which only remained popular for a short time, also stand in the Weimar tradition. But let us remember...

At the end of the First World War, when literature became increasingly rational and political, drama took on a leading role for the Expressionists. These artists were rebels who proclaimed ecstatically that a better society was (Vision creates Man), wrote Kaiser, and it was this vision of a new world, which dominated the first and "ecstatic" phase of German Expressionism. As a "tribune," a "tribunal" and a "place of worship," the theatre should serve the community of mankind,

---

*Key speech of the 1992 Louisville International Theatre Festival "The Golden 20ies."

"celebrate the cult of the human person," inspire "world-transforming deeds" and proclaim the beginning of the earthly paradise. For the Expressionists, it is a place of "ecstasy" and "magical communication" that should guide audiences to a "shared experience of the divine." The starting point for all change is the "revolution of the spirit." Roused by the power of the word, the individual can achieve the much-heralded "transformation" from the "bad" and "wicked enemy" to the "pure creature of light," from egoist to "fellow creature." The transforming of existing reality into an earthly paradise is achieved by multiplying such individual transformations. A programmatic process of this sort insures from the start that the "revolution of Expressionism," despite its intentions, remains within the realm of the ideal.

Playwrights like Walter Hasenclever (1890–1940), Georg Kaiser (1878–1945), Ernst Barlach (1870–1938) or Ernst Toller (1893–1939) surrendered the coordinates of external, primary reality for the sake of creating an artistic reality within which the idea can be freely unfolded. Verisimilitude, credibility, and psychology by the board; what matters is the creation of a new mythology. The process of separating the several arts from their traditional context and reducing them to their fundamental elements, a process initiated by Gordon Craig and Adolphe Appia in the course of the theatrical reforms around 1900, is now carried even further and radicalized. The new stage techniques refer to their emphasis on geometrical forms and "dramatic" lighting.

Another influence came from Antoine's *Theatre Libre* and the German *Stilbühne*, which stressed simplicity in staging as much as possible with props. Vasily Kandinsky (1866–1944) too, and thereby conjure up the "intellectual-spiritual," laid the groundwork with his program of "stage synthesis."

As I said, the Expressionists' ecstatic *Schrei* (Scream) is for "kindness, justice, comradeship, love of man for man…" because "the world begins in man and God is discovered as a brother" [37, p. 67]. Aufbruch (Departure/Awakening) became the catchword for the Expressionists' desire for transfiguration or moral regeneration. Georg Büchner's *Woyzeck* in the nineteenth century was an early ancestor of the new type of drama, and Strindberg's mystical visionary traits were adapted as well. Wedekind transformed these traits into critical-eccentric characteristics. With Strindberg, the early expressionist dramas found the exterior form of "synthetic image sequence." With Büchner, they found an example of fragment technique (Fetzentechnik). The expressionist plays were ballads in visionary image sequels which were depicted as Stations." "The Struggles of Man" and "Dramatic Message." Expressionist drama was generally done in lyrical-monologue style and distanced itself from the broad personal human spectrum, which is found in naturalism with its imitating style. The style of the Expressionists also differed greatly from the psychological symbolism of the impressionists. Avowals and confessions counted more for the Expressionists than conflicts did. Their heroes were mostly the mere likeness and mouthpiece of the poets.

At the time, the following was formulated as the task of the expressionist drama: "Instead of wanting to examine and analyze the temporal, we want to become aware of that which is extemporal within ourselves... and so her [in the expressionist drama] humans are nothing but spirit and soul, and therefore, there is something insane about these characters. Ecstatic and raving, they step out of the terrestrial thicket and yet are gifted with the true mark of humanity" [35, p. 17].

The major character in the expressionist drama was the youth. His protest was seldom aimed at an opponent (and when it was, the opponent was often embodied in father-figures) but rather directed against super-human powers. Realistic details and the bourgeois surroundings were of no avail. Information about name and social position were non-existent and listed in the bill of characters were often only "the man," "the son," "the yellow figure," etc. The characters were vehicles for ideas: "Through the characters, the mind grows up to the highest possibility" [37, p. 67]. Even the scenic notes were subject to abstract formulations: "Tensely, fearfully breaks out his paralyzation, sprouting unreal blossoms..." [37].

Of course this kind of drama demanded a new staging style. Music and sound were elevated to the status of performers and all stage machinery was openly included. The Expressionists tried to break through the barrier of illusion, which separated the audience from the stage. They brought the public into the ranks of revolutionary humanity. The theatre should no longer be just a mirror but rather the expression of contemporary life.

The tendency to abstract the human being as a vehicle for occurrences on stage reached its climax with the mechanical theatre of Bauhaus. The consequences such a character concept brought fro the performing arts are obvious: the renunciation of imitating reality and psychological nuances. The analytical psychological art of acting is replaced by a rhythmical structure. This holds true for the form of speech with its excesses, agglomerations, abbreviations and emotional superlatives, as well as for the body language. In comparison with naturalistic theatre, body language gains in great value for the Expressionists. Physicality as the "original source and exposing element" is the central criterion for expressionistic acting, above all, as realized by Werner Kraus (1884–1959), Fritz Kortner (1892–1970), Agnes Straub (1890–1941), Heinrich George (1893–1946) and Ernst Deutsch (1890–1969).

Rhythmical acting fins its corollary in the architectural set and stage. All space should be as neutral as possible in order not to dominate the actions and characters. The set often first obtains its meaning through the lighting. With the light changes, the rapid scene changes are accomplished as demanded by the "Station Drama." The lighting and spatial effects are often described in detail in the scenic directions. In the expressionist drama, the set is an "inner space" which has been turned outwards. Therein, objects are often treated as living beings. Set designers like Emil Pirchan (1894–1957), Cesar Klein (1876–1954), Otto Reigbert (1890–1957), and Ludwig Sievert (1887–1968) tried to accomplish such effects with the help of twisted perspectives and magical lighting effects.

Before the end of World War I, expressionist drama had just been tried out in a few private theatres, and with the collapse of the old regime it was half exemplary for the voice of the Weimar republican era and gained entrance into the subsidized municipal and state theatres. Directors such as Gustav Harting (1887–1946), Karl-Heinz Martin (1888–1948), Richard Weichart (1880–1961), Otto Falkenberg (1873–1947) and, above all, Leopold Jessner (1878–1956) had recognized the concepts of expressionist drama years earlier and used them in productions of the classics. Especially Jessner, now Intendant and director of the Preußisches Staatstheater, had employed expressionist principles of concentration, of scenic reduction, and of dynamic acceleration. Above all, his production of Schiller's *Wilhelm Tell* (1919) became famous as a "cry of freedom" on a simple stage with a staircase (later known as the Jessner staircase). This production shows Jessner's main principal that "the intention will absorb all details of performance and consequently all details of the set as well" [31, p. 21].

In a historically novel way, however, styles, struggle for political thrust, and economic concentration in and around Berlin theatre reflected an increasing aggravation of social confrontation in the center of the Weimar Republic. Along with Brecht's Epic Theatre and his *Lehrstücke* (didactic plays), the most important contributions to political theatre during the 20s, we find the productions of Piscator. Brecht and Piscator agreed that theatre not only may reflect the world but rather should also contribute to its change. "Mass appeal" was the key norm of their activities. This was done by pointing out moral codes and social norms. On the one hand, Brecht developed a new dramaturgy and a form of acting which "alienated" the occurrences of reality. Piscator, on the other hand, wanted to implant the events amongst the characters in their social and political surroundings (sociological dramaturgy) in order to escalate understanding and the agitation-effect in his audience, which was mostly not working but middle-class. Piscator conceived his theatre as epic and named it as such before Brecht had done so. Piscator's theatre operated with the help of documentation in collage form, and with costly technical apparatus. He had installed a conveyor belt on the front of the stage and a cantilever bridge in the center which could move up and down. Sections of the stage could rise or fall, revolve or slide. Lantern slides an film were projected. Above the proscenium arch blazed Communist slogans. Searchlights played on the audience; motorbikes roared on the stage; loudspeakers blared, drums reverberated, machines throbbed, armies tramped, crowds roared and machine guns rattled shrilly.

Brecht described Piscator's as the most radical attempt to endow the theatre with an instructive character. For Piscator the theatre was a parliament, the public a legislative body. His theatre collective synthesized and gave expression to a number of characteristics typical of the Berlin avant-garde of the 20s: The attack on established art, a gradual politicization of the art, and the belief in the beneficial influence that technology and the technological media — film and radio — would exert on the transformation of social values. Piscator's views on the heritage and future of literature and art were formed by his close connection to a group of people in Berlin, most of whom belonged to the dada movement: the brothers Herzfelde (Heartfield), George Grosz, Walter Mehring, Richard Hulsenbeck, Franz Jung, and Raoul Hausmann, some of whom became part of the theatre collective. In contrast to the Expressionists' individualist-humanist sentiments, the Berlin Dadaists emphasized a "cooling out" (*auskuhlen*) or "freezing" (*einfrosten*) of feelings in art and a radical anarchical destruction of bourgeois art under the slogan *"Kunst ist Scheiße"* (art is shit), which was quite shocking at that time. After the 1919 Spartacus (communist) uprising in Berlin, dada took a turn toward greater political articulation. It is in this context that Piscator conceived of theatre and art as a political tool, a means of pedagogy and propaganda. Under the slogan "Art is a Weapon," theatre workers led by Piscator lent shape and substance to the left-wing section of theatre in Berlin during that time.

There is no doubt: the continuing aesthetic innovation and its socio-political ambitions raised the expressionist cultural rebellion to a higher level of political cultural revolution. The diversity and productivity in this struggle made Berlin appear to be the theatre capital of the Golden Twenties.

Let's trace some major examples, each of them representing that variety and intensity of experimentation.

The premiere of Ernst Toller's *Die Wandlung. Das Ringen eines Menschen* (Transfiguration) took place on September 30, 1919, following the collapse of the old order. Yet Toller could not attend this event. His involvement in the Bavarian Soviet Republic earned him a sentence of five years imprisonment for treason in Munich in July 1919, and he was thus at the time incarcerated.

The critical echo to the Berlin premiere of Toller's play was in every respect one of approval. Willi Handl applauded: "That was an evening that will be inscribed on my memory" [14]. Ernest Heilborn stated: The poetic organization of this *Ringen eines Menschen* is such that the realism of each phase of experience merges directly with the symbolism of the entire occurrence [...] Intellectually this drama leads to the point where humanity takes the place of the concept of Fatherland; that the proletariat, here meaning the crucified, is issued the call to march, but only after having freed its humanity from within, becoming conscious that its enemies are its brothers. This drama has something of the mysterious darkness of cathedrals, yet out of the darkness emerges the human, the poet [23]. Siegfried Jacobsohn emphasized: "Toller's hatred is to the henchmen and hell-hounds, deaf to the people's cry for peace, at the rogues and riff-raff whose business is murder and who even, at the safe distance from the smoking gun, won't stop using murder to do business. [...] These villains, fattening themselves while the courageous activists rot away in dungeons, should be shown in their true colors every evening from every podium in every auditorium in every German city" [30].

The success of the Tribune performance carried far beyond Berlin. Many other theatres acquired the play for their repertory. Toller confirmed this from the prison in a letter, dated May 22, 1921: "*Die Wandlung* has appeared in 15 thousand copies. It was already performed in Berlin (about 115 times), in Hamburg (about 35 times), in Stuttgart and in Cologne. Further performances have been accepted in Vienna, Bruenn, Maehrisch-Ostrau, and Munich" [59, quoting Ernst Toller].

In Toller's drama, theatrical Expressionism became for the first time fulfillment instead of experiment. The decorations (by Robert Nepach) were pawns of suggestion. Freight train — and in front of the darkened curtain stood a medium-high piece of wall with barred windows; desert camp — and a painted campfire was there; chicken wire — and a small frame; an army hospital — and a whitewashed piece of wall was set up. The local motif of the scene was struck, and the various motifs were bound together and dissolved through alternate dimming and brightening of the lights. Before these abbreviated, loaded images, the players gave abbreviated, loaded performances. Words clumped rhythmically together and then broke apart. Cries rose and sank. Movements advanced and retreated. No psychology or development was presented here, but concentration and immediacy. Not drawing, but dotted images. Not gesticulation, but power. Photos showed that an assembly was determined not by masses of actors, but by accentuated groups.

All critics described that on that evening the theatre took a step forward. Herbert Ihering writes the next morning: "The Tribune won the right to its intention. How the individuals stood out against the suggestion of the whole! Bodies became ecstatic, moods explosive. A student (in the assembly scene) had such an intensity of listening and accompanying in chin and forehead, in eye and hand, that her speech was inevitably restrained. Herr Gotow, in playing the various forms of death, had such a sharp, precise, accentuated plasticity of the grotesque that he left his romanticized Reinhardt beginnings behind him. If director Karl Heinz Martin can be given sole credit for the organization, spacing, and loading of the scenes, then he has done an extraordinary job. He achieved the transformation of the objective into the demonic. He created concentrated silence and rigorous eruption. Always essence. Always expression" [28].

Toller's play forces the director to deal with scenic problems with which the normal stage would have difficulty coming to terms. Graves come alive, skeletons of soldiers rise from the graves, commune with one another, dance and speak ghostly unreality. Neppach's arabesque screens with their barbed wire proved a compelling and fantastic setting, while Martin mastered the comical dialogue of a screeching, scornful *danse macabre*. The audience felt convinced of the sound of clacking bones, saw skulls and rib cages, heard diabolical piping voices, all without the injurious intrusion of garish effects, the mood neither blunted by obvious intentions nor pierced with exaggerations. As one other witness of that premiere said: "This new style has the special virtue of keeping itself free of all antics" [29].

Famous for its new kind of visualization is Jessner's 1920 production of Shake-speare's *Richard III*. In an article written after the premiere, Jessner referred to the experiment of the staggered stage which, as in the *Wilhelm Tell* production, was also employed in the production of *Richard III*. Yet the same attempt to convey the idea of the play symbolically — instead of through historical reproduction — was even more apparently aspired to in *Richard III*. Here the terraced stage no longer functioned as an independent architectural elevation (as in *Tell*), but as an expression of the fateful course of events. Richard Gloucester is driven to the top of the red flight of steps where he is then crowned as Richard III. Then the battle scenes unfold. And on the same red steps where Richard the warrior stood at the pinnacle of his glory, half naked — torn, confused, a madman already — reeling from the highest height to the deepest depth, his downfall is consummated [31, p. 65].

Fritz Kortner, who played the title role and who in those years was Jessner's most important actor, maintained in his memoirs, *Aller Tage Abend*, that the basic concept for the production came from him. "Even in my boyhood fantasies," he wrote, "I always imagined 'Career' as the ascent of many steps — up to the most dizzying heights. And the fall from above was a child's nightmare. Thus I initially put my thoughts about a set design [...] on paper" [36, p. 352]. Kortner then describes the realization of the idea as follows: "Richard's fortune and fate should take place on the up- and downstairs action of the steps. At terrific speed, in gal-loping speech with slackened reins, biting pangs of conscience, trodding down people and other obstacles, Richard charges wildly on the upward to power. In every line this distant goal was apparent." The costumes did not present a picture of the times, nor did the sets reflect the color of the period. Everything was sub-ordinated to the will to power. Jessner, who, according to Kortner, was "a master of contraction, reduction, and succinct meaning" [36, p. 369], celebrated with this production one of the greatest triumphs of direction, and Kortner achieved as Richard one of this greatest performances as an actor.

To Polgar, he appeared in the Vienna guest performance as a "black titan. An executive agent of darkness. A demonic monster, let loose upon a rotting world in order to accelerate its decay. He is all of those things, only not a king," Polgar continued, "neither on the horizontal nor the steps. He remains a raging plebeian, a dark and base primitive. One can imagine the grass of graveyards growing in his treads" [45].

Most critics viewed Jessner's achievement with either unreserved praise or utter enthusiasm. Ludwig Sternau admired how Jessner gave "these scenes Hodler's style and Rembrandt's chiaroscuro, going boldly against all tradition as once before in the production of *Tell*" [52].

To Koeppen this production "was the greatest (and in many ways the most lasting) theatrical event in Berlin in years" [33]. Koeppen summarized his opinion in the following words: "If Reinhardt bestowed the Renaissance of Shakespeare as Comedy upon us, then the man who saves that was left to be saved of the Monumental Shakespeare is – despite all the rude commentary about him – Leopold Jessner!" [33]

But Expressionism could not have developed as it did without Reinhardt's pioneering theatrical style. By reviving Greek classics (*The Oresteia, Oedipus, Elektra* in Hofmannsthal's version), Reinhardt showed the viability of poetic drama on the modern stage and also restored the possibility of portraying generalized human struggle, of depicting representative figures in conflict with cosmic forces in place of the petty domesticity of much Naturalistic drama. Reinhardt in 1919 produced *The Oresteia of Aeschylus* in his newly built Grosses Schauspielhaus ("The Theatre of the Five Thousand"), which had an open stage and every possible contemporary mechanical device. It was Reinhardt's hope that his theatre would contain modern life as once the great arena had contained the Greek community. He borrowed freely from the technique of the circus and from the Chinese and Japanese theatres. It was his avowed intention to free the theatre from the shackles of literature. Every production was different, seeking the form within. "There is no one style or method," he affirmed. "All depends on realizing the specific atmosphere of the play, on making the play live" [47, p. 37]. He could be intensively theatrical, or he could take realism and charge it with poetry, thereby adding to it an extra dimension.

In his production of *The Dream*, although he used a realistic set, as the trees, hills and bushes of the forest moved on the revolve, revealing always new vistas, so the forest seemed vast and vibrant with magic. Reinhardt was a brilliant organizer of effects too, planning a production down to the smallest detail.

His *Regiebuch*, the prompt copy, was even more detailed than the shooting script of a film. Reinhardt not only removed the fourth wall; he helped to remove the second wall as well — the painted wall at the back. It was Reinhardt who in the early years of this century introduced the extension of the stage to the rear. This flight of steps to the rear of the stage not only created the possibility of entering from the rear; he also emphasized such entrances by providing a staircase to lead down to the stage.

But his was the theatre of identification. There was never any doubt in his mind that a performance had to compel an audience to forget their everyday selves and to accept the play, while it lasted, as the only meaningful reality. He always compared actors to children "whose games are truly creative ... They transformed themselves at once into whatever they see, and transform everything into whatever they wish" [47]. A whole generation of great German actors and actresses who, at that time, made Berlin that theatrically exciting city, would never have found their "own melody," "their deepest self," without Reinhardt's incomparable gift to divine and absorb the individuality of actors he worked with. The Expressionist's blatant aesthetic contrasted with Reinhardt's love of subtlety. He rejected the *Schrei* in favor of the gentle modulated voice. The Expressionist's revolutionary idealism affronted Reinhardt's gentle humanism. While Reinhardt celebrated the special quality of individuals and their relationships, the Expressionists were committed to the portrayal of "universal Man."

A disciple of Reinhardt was Erwin Piscator, who, as I mentioned earlier, invented the "documentary theatre." In December 1927 he began work on an adaptation for the stage of Hasek's novel *The Good Soldier Schweik*. Besides him Brecht, George Grosz, Felix Gasbarra, and Leo Lania were involved in this production. The ambitious innovative mechanized environment shows the ingenious solution to the problem of movement. The character of Schweik is seen in constant senseless motion of which he is not the originator but only the object. Moreover, for all his moving around he remains essentially passive and unchanging. Piscator had the brilliant idea of placing the Schweik actor, Max Pallenberg, on a conveyor belt built level with the stage floor to illustrate the character's stasis within motion.

Projections of film footage taken as tracking shots in the actual streets of Prague alternated with animation film of a political satirical nature by George Grosz. Grosz also did backdrop drawings and designs (about three hundred pages) for masks and costumes (all of which resulted in a blasphemy trail against him and his publisher). Inspired by the political, grotesque marionettes that Heartfield and Grosz had done earlier for dada, Piscator decided on a whole range of marionettes to surround Schweik, from totally artificial puppets to actors with masks or simply mechanical, robot-like acting. Grosz also credits Piscator with introducing photomontage into the framework of the stage, and claims that Piscator's theatre – which today would be called a multimedia spectacle, since Piscator also worked with slide shows, music, dance, and pantomime in addition to film and puppets – was an expression of his "Wagner yearnings," his never-ending search for the great *Gesamtkunstwerk* that would comprise all the individual arts [50, p. 107]. Grosz's remark is interesting, especially in light of Brecht's later partial rejection of Piscator's efforts.

To realize his ideological aims, Piscator began to envisage a *Total theater*. The execution of the design was to be in the hands of the Bauhaus. Like the Bauhaus artists, he was deeply convinced that the purpose and function of a building should dictate for form. All technical means, both Piscator and Gropius (the architect) argued, are employed to abolish the bourgeois stage arrangement and replace it with a form that "no longer considers the audience a fictive concept, but includes it into the theater as a live force." For this purpose stages were arranged not only to jut out from the proscenium into the center of the audience, as is common in most modern theatres, but to surround the spectators on all sides as well. In addition to the horizontal distribution of stage levels, a vertical spread of stage areas was made possible by moveable staircases and scaffolds. Gropius further admitted that his special interest was directed at the various methods of light projection demanded by Piscator's general *mise-enscene*. These light projections meant both the creation of scenic-dramatic space — the building of a scene with light as replacement for props and sets — and also the projection of film and slides on as many surfaces as possible — walls, ceilings, and so on — in order to submerge the audience in the heightened illusion of being present at the actual site of scenic events.

Now that he had his own theatre (paradoxically in the West End of Berlin), Piscator established a Studio, a collective of authors, actors, dramaturges, directors, musicians and technicians working together on selected projects. The Studio offered acting classes which included training in stylistics, foreign languages, theatre history, stage sets, costume and film-making. As you know, Piscator would later continue it in the form of the Dramatic Workshop, which he established in New York in 1940 and which was attended by such artists as Tennessee Williams, Marlon Brando, Rod Steiger, Walter Matthau and Tony Curtis.

In opposition to the majority of the expressionist cultural rebels, Bertolt Brecht did not advocate aesthetic means or dramaturgical techniques, but rather a method of theatrical representation based on a particular way of viewing the world. Brecht wanted to see a theatre that would satisfy the spectator's "naïve" need for entertainment, his curiosity about the world, his appetites for fun and excitement. Brecht's theatre concept intends to bring the audience pleasure by helping them understand social and political reality and motivate them to enter into that world and transform that. From a famous line of Karl Marx — that until now philosophers have only interpreted the world, but the real task is to change it — Brecht derived the most important dictum for his Epic Theatre: Show man and society on the stage as changing and changeable. Thus his works were directed at the contemporary public, "which eats today's beef today," as he formulated it in an essay in 1926.

The early play *Baal* (1919) is a prologue for Brecht: the new linguistic strength of his poetry proclaims itself here as well as his program for the theatre. If we look at Baal's "appetite," his desire for happiness, then we should always bear in mind how it functions in the historical process as well. This is the sensualists revolutionary who has been lost, who is always lost, if we stagnate in the revolt itself. Baal forfeits the consent of established society, enters as an outsider and compels an educated, affluent society to pay up. Theatre against the norm and completely without social consent achieves the desired shiver of a sellout: theatre as immoral institution. Baal's schemes, his attempts to come out of his isolation, are passed off by society as being harmless, in as much as society sanctions them. Baal is "on the road" but to make our planet "habitable." Baal's erotic and sexual activity comes from his isolation in a society that produces the "Dehumanized masses." Can he be blamed for seeing himself under poisonous skies? Brecht wrote in 1921: "That is the coldness that you find in your heart."

After the Berlin production of *Man is Man* (1928) — in which soldiers were made to appear as scarecrows and monstrosities by means of half masks, giant hands, stilts and wire frames under over-sized uniforms — Brecht had already gathered, after nearly ten years of work in the theatre, all essential tools for his new stage. The hard capitalism in the Weimar Republic brought him, by way of a "work-related accident," to Marxism: while doing research for a play, he examined the trading on the grain exchange, he could not proceed with a study of Marx's *Kapital*. This reading had a profound effect on his work. Brecht henceforth presented to a far greater degree man's behavior as being determined by social conditions, "We'd rather be good, instead of so raw/ But conditions are not like that." Brecht says in the famous chorus of "The Uncertainty of Human Conditions" in

The Threepenny Opera. This theme of man's inherent schizophrenia, which arises from the desire to be good and the frustration of this by social conditions, appears in many of his following plays. As one critique has put it: "The irrational anarchist had submitted himself to the murderous discipline of a rational doctrine of salvation" [50, George Grosz, p. 145]. Brecht never again tested the foundations of his truth; his only concern henceforth was to formulate and proclaim it in a different way.

The criminals in *The Threepenny Opera* (premiere on August 31, 1928, Theater am Schiffbauerdamm, Berlin) behave like middle-class citizens in order to force the audience to the following conclusion: since criminals are successful because of their middle-class manners and methods, these manners and methods themselves must be criminal. Yet no one thought to extract this social criticism. On the contrary, the middle-classes took with culinary gusto to the cynically formulated, enchantingly insolent songs composed by Weill and even collaborated to turn them into hits: "First comes the chow, then the morality." *The Threepenny Opera* made Brecht a celebrity overnight. A second infusion followed only one year later: *Happy End* (premiere August 31, 1929). This Chicago gangster spectacular, with the Salvation Army lieutenant Halleluja Lilian, the predecessor of St. Joan of the slaughterhouses, contained one bit of anti-capitalistic spite. When the gangsters enter the Salvation Army in closed ranks, they do so with the following realization: "What's a picklock in comparison to a share, what's a break-in in comparison to the establishment of a bank!" Works of this period more rich in invention and wit are *The Rise and Fall of the City of Mahagonny* (1928/29, and opera composed by Kurt Weill) and *St. Joan of the Slaughterhouse* (1929/30), but they too belong to Brecht's "Agitprop" minded period of revolutionary activism.

Just to give you one very clear example of Brecht's didactic work (*Lehrstück*), the worst but formally the finest piece in this series is *The Precaution* (premiere December 10, 1930 by the worker's chorus of greater Berlin). Four revolutionaries, sent by Moscow to China, have shot a young Chinese comrade, and they present their case in front of the *Kontrollchor*, that is, the party tribunal, as "theatre within the theatre." The comrade was guilty because he yielded to the human impulses of pity, outrage and anger instead of agitating in compliance with the party's orders, avoiding conflicts with the police and ingratiating himself with the profiteer with whom the party wishes to form an alliance. When he tears up his mask, which symbolically indicates that he has sacrificed his individuality for the party and is but an empty page upon which "the revolution writes its instructions," he is shot and thrown into a chalk pit. The *Kontrollchor* tribunal permits this "precaution," and even the young comrade consented to it shortly before his death, "in the interest of communism... saying yes to the revolutionizing of the world." Prophetic Brecht! Five years later, during the Moscow trials, the old guard of the revolution was prepared in terms of this very paradigm to acquiesce to its own execution.

These few but different examples underline how the Weimar era should not be approached narrowly and formalistically. To be an avant-garde is truly to be way out in front. It was a "time of rebellion" and "confusion," as Brecht says in the poem *To Posterity*, written in the late 1930's. He then was already in exile, and the "Golden 20th" seemed to be once and forever past: "Expressionism" as well as "political theatre," Reinhardt, Jessner, Toller, Brecht, Piscator and many other people who created that most innovative period became victims of the Nazi regime, fleeing Germany or filling the concentration camps. Much that was foreseen by the Weimar pioneers has come to pass during the twelve years abroad — mainly in the United States. After 1945 European and world theatre has gradually re-discovered the Weimar heritage. With the liberation of middle and eastern Europe new horizons are opening. But even today the value of these works of course depends on the use which posterity makes of them. To experiment is to make a foray into the unknown — it is something that can be charted only after the event.

29 Necessity versus Progress: Does Ancient Greek Theatre Provide a Vehicle to Guarantee Equal Rights or Does It Simply Imply a Virtuous System?*

1 Athenian democracy was based on the right of her citizens to express themselves in public and to execute civil responsibility and solidarity. The most magnificent and lasting testimonial to this is Greek theatre.

When Greek, German, American, Cypriot and Japanese theatre artists were working together on Sophocles' *Antigone*[1] in 1986 at the Ancient Greek theatre ruin of Oeniades near Messolongiou – in their very different languages and coming from different cultural roots and social and political backgrounds – we were drawn, bit by bit, into the spectacle of an unexpected, inconclusive turn of the play's events. Thus it is obvious from Sophocles' attitude towards "tragic myth" that one of the things he found in it, one of the powerful holds on the actors and their audience, was the authority of what we would call "history." For the fifth century Athenians, their vision of past, of their own history, was poetic from the start, its personages and events symbolic representations of every aspect of Man's life on earth, his strength and weakness in the struggle against his fellow men, the forces of nature, and the bleak fact of his own mortality.

The masked actors in the theatre of Dionysus presented to the audience not only the historical figures of the hearsay past but also its own ambitions and its fate, its social cohesion. [18, p. 76]

What characterized man, Greeks felt, was his *rationality* and so their theatre stressed, in re-writing the myth as well as in performing the story, the process of reasoning and the uses of reason to modify or control instinct and will. *Self-*

---

*Paper presented at the 10th conference of ISSEI in cooperation with the University of Malta, held at Valetta, July 24–30, 2006.

[1] First produced bilingual (Modern Greek/English) by the International Workshop for Ancient Drama Inc. (Directors Heinz-Uwe Haus, Nicos Shiafkalis) and the International Workshop and Study Center for Ancient Drama (President Stelios Tsitsimelis) for the re-opening of the Ancient Greek theatre of Oeniades (Messolongiou/Greece) with the help of the village community of Catochi and the Archaeological Service of Patras on September 2, 1986; re-produced with the 1987 ensemble in English translation by Paul Roche (premiere June 27, 1987) again in Oeniades, guest performances 1987 and 1988 in Greece and Cyprus. In all three productions the black New York actress Robyn Hatcher played the title role.

examination was vital to their *polis'* "social contract"; the unexamined life was not worth living, said Socrates. An unexamined life revealed the need for *order, proportion* and *restraint*. These guidelines for the social being became the training tools for democratization of the community — nothing in excess.

Compromise building and collective agreement by implementing mechanisms that are geared towards delivering justice. These cautions, however, were not intended to restrain the human urges for *arete,* or excellence; the final goal of intelligent living was to realize one's full potential, in body and mind. The ideal of "civil society" was the driving force for the "realization of civil rights."

Whether or not, or how far, Ancient Athens could be fairly called a democracy, with its disenfranchised women and social classes, depends on the use and definition of terms and the ability of us to historize arguments and facts as well. It also depends on our capacity to embrace the driving force of contradictions. For example, it is a fact that attempts were made by the Council of 500, onto which, by a whole series of stratagems, the better off seemed to enrich themselves, to impose a form of guidance which constituted political control, but they were never wholly successful. The Ecclesia met less frequently, and its votes rarely counted, and decisions demonstrated by a general show of hands. It was swayed by emotional oratory as much as rational argument. And we know there is some evidence that, at the height of democracy in Athens, the poorer classes still seemed to have "loved a Lord": Alcibiades was given a high state office because his team of horses won at the Olympic games. But that and other facts should not really be questions to argue about. Far more important than the question of voting was the concept of *isonomia,* or equality before the law. This protected the poorer classes for a century against the oppression of the well-to-do. It was an idea which had not occurred to any previous society and which was, in practice, rejected by most subsequent ones. The greatness of Athens lies in her having conceived and, for a time, nurtured such an ideal.

And it is this Greek ideal, which stands behind the 18th century Enlightenment vision, in which legislation and education are fused as the source of democratic wisdom. This classic tradition is still dominating today's political thought: "legislation and education are the building blocks for democracy." [27, p. 116]

2   Ancient Greek drama teaches that individual ability and the freedom to change the direction of events through political involvement — without incurring a re-

taliatory backlash from the state — is critical to democracy. Historizing their own mythological contexts meant for the Athenian audience re-evaluating its "use value" for their actual needs as a community. The re-writing of pre-historic stories led directly to dynamic social exchange between the drama onstage and the drama of life outside the *theatron*, the "seeing place." The temporal exigencies of performance are *ad hoc* playgrounds, engaging in questions of moral, political and religious authority, each moment significant and yet unrecoverable. The dramaturgy is always strictly the same: a known series of incidents that precipitates a crisis and brings the meaning of the protagonist's actions into focus, has to be judged for the *polis'* policymaking. Aristotle termed, as we know, this crisis the *peripeteia*, or reversal, and he argued that it should be accompanied by an act of *anagnorisis*, or recognition, in which the character responds to this change. Aside from the ongoing speculations about reversal and recognition and the functioning of *catharsis* or the impact the emotional pressures, the performed tragic actions may have raised for the audience. In our context it can be taken for sure, that the *parabasis*, the choral ode known from Aristophanes' plays, delivered to the audience discussing political issues, must have been the most provoking theatrical invention, replacing earlier choral dancing and revelry. The need to replace older viewing habits through "thinking capable of intervention" is not an invention of the 20th century theatre revolution. It was a basic attitude in the emerging of the theatre's social function.

The right of Athens' citizens to express themselves in public implies that a democracy goes beyond the freedoms of street mobilization or electoral participation and also requires the building of democratic institutions. What can be more true to contemporarythought than facts like this? From Baghdad to Gaza we experience institution building that provides the base for democratizing the minds of the people. Since Pericles, the main challenge is the maintenance of democracy as a universal concept rather than a nationalist belief based on special conditions for democracy predicated on racial, religious or local criteria. There should be no doubt that this is an extreme actual aspect for re-reading Ancient Greek drama and its conditions of existence. It goes directly to the heart of parochial claims with its counterclaim that culture is a universal frame of reference when it comes to politics. "No," teaches Ancient Athens, and EU-Brussels is as wrong as the mullahs Teheran or Peking's claim. "Depriving democracy of its singularity and insisting upon its conception as one part of a paired hyphen, such as Egyptian, Russian or American democracy, mocks the notion of effective participation and enlightened understanding. It reduces democracy to special and particular footnote to nationalism." [27, p. 115]

Democracy may appear to be just a set of institutions, courts, congresses, laws and constitution; but those are facilities that emerge from actions and attitudes lodged in the hearts and minds of average people over a long period of training. The performances of Ancient Greek drama were one essential factor of this process. *Order, proportion* and *restraint* are social and political guidelines, which transformed into expressions of the *ethos*.

3   The orchestra with its chorus narrating and spectators listening, offered ideal training grounds for a new value system of commitments and obligations. Tolerance, or putting up with ideas of others; the legitimacy of democratic institutions, or accepting responsibility undertaken by legal processes; belief in the equality of all people; compromise, or the ability to accept defeat as part of the democratic process — are social attitudes which had been trained in Ancient Athens. It is this ideal we can learn from for a culture of democracy, which we need as urgently in a time of globalization, with democracies still the minority in the world, as Athens needed it in its confrontation with Sparta. The "winds of progress," to use an expression of hope from 1920s politicized theatre in Europe, came not just to a standstill soon after that time. They never really recovered from history's bloody reality. So if we talk and accept the notion of culture as central to democracy, we should return the debate to its 19th century roots in Kant and Hegel, where one must choose between the free conscience and the well-ordered state. The balancing of rights and obligations becomes the grounds for democracy in a well-ordered state. Many 20th century nations were "well-ordered states," but neither in Moscow, Berlin, nor Rome did citizens have a say or stand equal before the law.

In turn, that leads to considerations which go further back than even Kant and Hegel into the less abstract world of Hobbes, Smith and Locke – a world in which democratic values fare less well and specific forms of justice fare better. Older notions were predicated on toleration and *laissez-faire* concepts of law that allowed a common starting point to all citizens. Here we may see a seed of a "civil society," which is not a cultural formation but a democratic functioning and communication. Both the Ancient Protagonist's and their chorus, like Pericles with his *polis,* had the same stage and audience conditions: unsparing in its insistence that democracy is not a bargaining exchange between classes, but an imposition on those who hold power and those who lack power. Any social contract – the one of Rousseau's Utopia or "The American Way of Life" – imposes social justice in order for democracy to prevail under one condition: *isonomia,* equality before the law. Of course, with the exception of the idea of "democratic equality" as "the principle of equal participation," that says little about the machinery of governance. But we may imagine an implicitly virtuous system the Athenians were striving for.

It associates an *ad hoc* approach to policymaking only too familiar to us in our time. Studying the functional value of Ancient Greeks performance in the theatre and in creating and executing law and order, we are left with a political vision of democracy as a process, similarly needed and practiced by today's Western democracies. The need for democracy's survival is a vision similar to ours "that would like to ensure a world of friendship based on abstract premises of the good society but in practice undulates between different ideologies and provides no real blueprint for action." [27, p. 117]

The current policy of the EU or the US, when it comes to dealing with dictatorships or measures to be taken in backing democratic change, appears to be so *ad hoc* that it lacks a degree of coherence and guiding principles.

The fundamental difference is that the Greeks believed in a universal principle which reconciled the forces of creation and destruction. They called it *moira,* translated variously as fate or *necessity.* To the modern mind, *necessity* is an unfamiliar idea. We believe instead, in progress – the idea that we can assert ourselves unconditionally and that, some day in the future, we will triumph once and for all over the forces of denial. The fascination in reading Ancient Greek tragedy, however, is in reading it as if we believed that our being cannot be asserted unconditionally, and that we occupy a small place in an immense universe in which all things, even the immortal gods, are subject to one force, *necessity.* It is the recognition of *necessity,* in one form or another, that finally resolves the conflict in Greek tragedy.

4   The "use value" of theatre was that it not only illustrated the result of the recognition, but became a tool for the *polis* to internalize the needs for the very basic conflict avoidance. It is only in the performance as we know that driving

motions, relationships, and events enclosed in the text are released to stimulate the audience members to reexamine their own contemporary events and relationships. Let us return to the example I mentioned earlier, the 1986 production of *Antigone* at Oeniades.[2]

By transforming the familiar into the unfamiliar, by making the habitual and customary seem strange and unexpected, Sophocles wanted to stimulate his audience to ask questions, to stand back from the stage actions and wonder about what they saw there. Rather than accepting the actions of a character as inevitable, the spectator in Sophocles' theatre is stimulated to question: Does it have to be this way? Has it always been so? Will it always remain so? What we discovered was that his theatre does deliver answers ready-made, but it asks questions, demanding that the audience enter into the stage events with its critical rather than apologetic faculties. Remember how the chorus is introduced by greeting the morning sun (beginning with verse 100) and how soon it becomes evident that the morning radiance of nature stands for the first day of peace: the Argives retreated the night before. The war is over. The town is free, and the citizens are freed from their fears. But even more: Nike, the goddess of victory has triumphantly bent to the side of the Thebans. So the elders of the town have come to announce the celebration of victory, Bacchus is to rule over Thebes for days and nights to come. Strikingly, the chorus does not at all lament the disastrous fate of Oedipus' sons and together with this the end of the Oedipus dynasty. After all, Oedipus once freed the town from the Sphinx, later from the plague. What is also striking is that Creon's enthronement, which is now legal, does not play any role for the chorus after the death of the brothers. Both facts are only mentioned briefly and without emphasis.

Does this imply that the citizens of Thebes are not interested in the events happening in the ruling dynasty, in who actually is their ruler, or in state affairs at all? Have they become sick of the long-lasting quarrels? Or are they furious about the scandalous Oedipus clan and glad to be relieved of their burden? Or are they just unable to realize what state affairs are and that they should be concerned by them? Or are they simply indifferent, because the prevailing power structure

---

[2] The company participated in the three symposia of the International Workshop and Study Center for Ancient Drama (IWSC): Ancient Drama as a Transcultural Event (August 25 – September 7, 1986, Agrinion, Greece), Ancient Tragedy and Contemporary View Habits (June 24 – July 2, 1987, Oeniades, Greece), Cultural Heritage and Politics (July 24/25, 1987, Nicosia, Cyprus).

prevents them from having an influence? Is what they want just peace and a happy life? How important is the proclaimed bacchanal feast for them; how much does peace mean to them, and what kind of peace is this? [18, p. 78]

Many other questions may arise in this context. They prove that the text can be applied to our contemporary world, which poses similar questions. For example, we see the weakening of civil responsibility and solidarity as one of the main threats to modern mass democracy. The future tasks of European societies could be described with three catchwords: civil society, community and Europe.

The concepts of "civil society" and "community" also take into account the events in Eastern Europe during the 1980's. In a remarkable reversal of the direction of influence, it was from there that the concept "civil society" returned to the Western European debate. But what could be seen as something dramatically new was in fact nothing more than democratic society with the liberal institutions of a constitutional state based on a free market economy. Some of you may remember that the Left was using the concept of civil society unacceptably as an antithesis to the concept of the liberal constitutional state. They were transforming the idea of civil society into an ersatz ideology of the Left. But with history as the winner, in the long term "communities based on old origins and traditions" would permeate the nation as the "solely effective framework for the realization of civil rights" and the deepening of integration. The Europe of Maastricht became the opportunity to realize this equilibrium of identities in an institutional way. Accession and integration into the EU were the results of legislation and education. Democratic wisdom was achieved through the right of new Europe's citizen's to express themselves in public.

The crucial question that free citizens face is what future role Europe will be able to play within the global context. Our situation is not so different to that of the Athenians *vis a vis* Sparta and its declared "cultural war" against democracy. Pericles' famous speech about his city as model for Hellas comes to mind: "Its administration favors the many instead of the few; this is why it is called a democracy. If we look to the laws, they afford equal justice to all in their private differences; if to social standing, advancement in public life fall to reputation for capacity, class considerations nor being allowed to interfere with merit; nor again does poverty bar the way." [54, p. 64]

Athens' civil rights, where public and private interests were not antagonistic contradictions, but a unit fostering human conditions, are another point of reference for Brussels and Strasburg:

> *Our public men have, besides politics, their private affairs to attend to, and our ordinary citizens, though occupied with the pursuits of industry, are still fair judges of public matters; for, unlike any other nation, regarding him who takes no part in these duties not as unambitious but as useless, we Athenians are able to judge at all events if we cannot originate, and instead of looking on discussion as a stumbling block in the way of action, we think it an indispensable preliminary to a wise action... [54, p. 64]*

The success or failure of the EU will certainly not only be decided by Europeans' "approval" of the global context, but also, ultimately, whether this Europe is able to survive against the global competition. It is only secondary by comparison, whether this aim will be achieved through the hegemony of a single nation or by means of other institutional structures. As Panayiotis Kondylis [34] underscores, the most important question is, what kind of political entity the extended Europe will be able to form. What counts is its identity, created in Ancient Athens democracy: "We are rather a pattern to others than imitators ourselves..." [54, p. 78] No doubt a lasting testimonial to this is its drama and theatre.

30 Between Symbol and Reality – a foreword to a new book about Yeats*

Whenever Yeats comes to mind, I cannot help thinking of four other Irish writers, Synge, O'Casey, Beckett, and Behan: disparate though they may seem, they are clearly linked through their explosive language, powerful and original images, unbridled imagination, passionate love of words, fiery joie de vivre, as well as their predilection for fairy tale wonders, the cruelty of the grotesque, and the shiver-inducing uncanny. Their theatrical creations are — in a Brechtian sense — gestural: their writing subverts the language of the oppressors even as it enhances it. This literary quintet reminds us that modern Western theater came about once writers discovered the poetic potential of social reality: in Paris the "Theatre Libre," in Berlin the "Verein Freie Bühne" — and in Dublin, chief city of a British

---

*Foreword (translated by Mark Harman) in [38].

colony, the "Irish National Theater Company," which Yeats helped to found in 1902. The "Naturalism" of this European movement, which ushered in the moderns, revolutionized all previous notions of how theater could be staged and what it might accomplish. To cite some names: Stanislavski, Georg von Meiningen, Gerhart Hauptmann and Arthur Schnitzler, Ibsen, Pasetti and Pallenberg — these actors, set designers, playwrights and directors discovered a form of social realism which changed for all time the craft of the theater and the nature of playgoing. These pioneers possessed an intimate knowledge of the soul and a love of humanity, especially of the poor and the oppressed, which gave the theater a freedom of interpretation that allowed it to assert itself and show its mettle.

What captivates me about Fred Lapisardi's observations is this opportunity to witness afresh the birth of the modern concept of theater, which continues to reverberate into the present. His accounts of Yeats's reception history offer a model for art and morality that has lost little of its relevance. It can stir interest in a potential liveliness in the theater, which may seem unimaginable to many contemporaries, for they have never experienced it themselves. How could things be any different, for, (at least in Germany,) the dominant directors seem like hirelings imported from the tabloids. (They are often the very people who once repeated their homicidal fantasies by rote out of Guevara's green book or Mao's red Bible) Those who cannot acknowledge that the possession of cultural identity entails a certain historical and social *parti pris* must inevitably capitulate to the pressures of a globalizing world and end up producing work that is senseless and always at the beck and call of the dominant ideology. Yeats's work could be the mirror that unmasks the distortions of contemporary theater.

What are these Yeatsian weapons which Lapisardi describes so competently and enthusiastically? Yeats succeeds in wresting from art its secrets without destroying its mysteries. As a result, his work clearly has a bearing on the current global cultural conflicts and it is even possible to regard his world of fantasy as a possible form of resistance. In his theatrical work the great Irishman knows how to make use of storytelling and engaged thought. Lapisardi's title evokes not the past but the utopian ideal of a stageworthy Yeats. As a result, the account we get here can be seen as a protest against the aesthetic exhaustion currently afflicting the western stage. In providing us with this "complementary perspective," Lapisardi no more vaunts his case than does Yeats himself when he discloses the unsettling thoughts prompted by the Noh-Theater. Following reverentially in Yeats's footsteps, the scholar adopts the playwright's faith in the increasing self-confidence of the public. We are encouraged to remain conscious of the context and to head in a direction leading away from the chaotic free-for-all of contemporary theater and harkening back to the collective experience which began at Thespis and by no means ended with Brecht. Lapisardi succeeds in establishing – to borrow a Brechtian term – the "use value" of Yeats for Paris, Berlin and Dublin (and the rest of the Western world!). And I know this from my own experience as a director.

In Germany, the stages that once stood for the world are now occupied by a would-be leftist army, composed of egocentric theatrical despots, directors hostile to the public and authors stuck in puberty, who terrorize the public with the excesses of their vacuity and their revulsion at life. For them the future is already worn-out; they have no screen onto which to project collective wishes, since they refuse to acknowledge the essential waywardness of art. Notorious for their contempt for democracy, they consider theater a secondary terrain, for their primary target is none other than the democratic system.

The western image of man, to which Yeats could still bear witness in the twentieth century for it was still in touch with its origins, stands alone against the prevailing destructiveness. In and of itself, it constitutes a humane rejection of deconstruction and randomness. It represents an existential truth which can be a mighty plaidoyer for the art of the theater. But in his texts – and this makes him an ally of such disparate contemporaries of Yeats as Kafka or Brecht – which contain numerous defamatory words, he plumbs the utter vulnerability of the mind when confronted with reality with a certain prickliness and anger but without the slightest complacency. It's as though Kafka's aphorism about the need for an axe "for the frozen sea within us" had made Yeats realize his own impotence. His webs of words are perceptible also in the aphorisms of the Augsburg star-gazer, whose *Keuner* stories unravel, disclosing – even in Dublin – a godless doubt about the power of language. It would be a grievous loss if we should fail to recognize the acuteness of perception released through Yeats's work. It's worth recalling that his plays opened a critical dialogue between art and ritual at a time when those murderous social experiments in Russia, Italy and Germany were not only in full swing but held much of Europe in thrall, a time, in other words, when the furies of oblivion threatened all attempts to assimilate "engaged thought."

In an age preoccupied with the dismantling of the self Yeats, who affirmed life with theatrical rigor, seems like a monument to tolerance. Ultimately, the challenge of his fables resides in their aesthetic form. One of Fred Lapisardi's strengths is that he makes it plain to readers that we cannot deal with plays, stories and myth in a haphazard fashion since man is a congenitally self-interpreting creature and, if his traditions and images are stripped away, he is lost. One can regard Yeats as a great exemplar of the human qualities inherent in the world of symbols--whoever destroys that world is left with a freedom that is purely negative and devoid of images.

At a time when many national theaters in Europe have degenerated into bone-yards of perversity the vision of the unicorn can serve as an emblematic stage direction for the rehearsals of the future. Let us recall the specifics: Wagner's young apprentice sets out to destroy the existing order so as to create a paradise of the "glowing land" on earth. He is joined by beggars and tramps, who steal and burn all before them. Before being killed by constables, he discovers that he has not understood his "voices" properly: his mission is not to "destroy, but to reveal." This underscores the grace attainable through the exertions of peaceful change.

Fred Lapisardi's book informs us about an artistic oeuvre which is said to be obsolete but, once it is staged, it can shake up those who have become deadened. Drawing on stories and history, he gives us an impression of the "Irish Renaissance" which could not have spread its faith in the real possibility of bringing about change in man and in society were it not for Yeats's Celtic thirst for salvation and his theatrical folk poetry.

I hope that Fred Lapisardi's book will attract many readers, for only those who are willing to learn and grow are capable of dispensing with those proselytizing pamphleteers who stand about on street corners.

31 The Tragic Sense of Life or We are left with self*

1   There is nothing new about the fact that the modern self tries to reread the past in terms of its present situation. This is unusual only in the intensity with which it is done. The impact of the 1989 revolution in Middle and Eastern Europe and the challenges of a worldwide globalization since then are, no doubt, current motivating factors. ("Porodicne Price" (Familiengeschichten Belgrad) by Biljana

---

*Paper presented at the Ninth International Symposium on Ancient Greek Drama, held at Droushia, Paphos, Cyprus, August 30 – September 2 2006.

Srbljanovic is such an all -European theme after the fall of the wall.) But the phenomenon in general is still directly related to the horrors of the two World Wars and the *hybris* of communist and national socialist/fascist experimentations of the 20th century and their lasting impact on Western self-determination. Those events had the double function of separating man from time and eliminating most associations with ordinary reality. The strategy of adjustment to unrestrained violence took in the 1920th the form of making unintelligible generalizations by defending it as something vast, unreal, and unavailable to rational explanation or as the outcome of certain circumstances. The balance between life, death and universality seemed not longer maintainable. How could one know, "what constitutes me most fundamentally" [46], Bernhard Reich asked in his 1927 Moscovite lectures about "Community in Classical Athens". From the ecstatic cry of the expressionists to the martial joy of being among the cadres of party discipline appeared as a result of man's free will, taken in the face of the "world's absurdity". It involved the most fundamental question of how man views and defines himself, and thus can assume the significance of modern myth.

Rejection of plots and dramatic situations in theatre became a characteristic means of representation of modern man in those years (as realized in the plays of Kaiser and Toller for example). "Great characters" became the focus of dramaturgy. A quest for disharmony, tension, the shocking, and the power of creating the fantastic were other traits of the expressionist mind (Artaud, Piscator). A wide-spread, quasi natural reaction to this movement was to trust nothing that is vague, abstract, and not associated with immediate experience. The evolution of Brecht's dramatic theory from his early rejection of Stanislavskian realism and his demanding of emotional coolness from the spectator to his later acceptance of the power of theatre to emotionally involve the audience reflects, on the one hand, his vivid awareness of the social and political events, but at the same time, orients itself along the ancient Greeks (and the Elisabethans). Simultaneously, the new middle class had been looking for an inspiration in developing an art form that would celebrate the community rather than the individual. The virtues of Homeric heroes and the widespread post-war trauma were interlinked and had made the public vulnerable to any new interpretation of its social and historical interests. Fascism, for example, "tapped the rebellious rejection of the young outsiders of a generation that had come of age in the trenches of war or in the street demonstrations and unemployment lines of the immediate postwar days. Mussolini's *squadristi* marched off singing *Giovinezza* (Youth). Captain Goemboes was thirty-three in 1920; Codreanu was twenty; Hitler thirty-one." [44, p. 212] Nazis and Communists alike considered the existing cultural system, the "Golden 20ies", so corrupted by the ruling classes, that it was beyond reform by even the most radical means; it could only be destroyed and replaced. However, it took until the "total capitulation" of the Third Reich and its allies in 1945 that the "theatre of character" was finally replaced by a "theatre of situation". Most collaborators of the nazis re-wrote their biographies and turned themselves into resistance fighters or innocent bystanders. Protagonists, who understood the *Zeitgeist*, stepped back into the chorus. To be a victim became the identity of the day, and the term "guilt" was unheard of. The famous Sartre/Camus controversy about the pendulum effect in history between societies based on religion and those based on man's challenges, up to this day still determines the ways of interpreting history and tragedy. The Greeks' portrayal of the heroic individual in conflict with the interests of the *polis* does not stand in sharp contrast to the radiating power of the existentialists. Sartre, in his "Forger des mythes" (1946), for instance, persuades the survivors of the "national-socialist experiment" to return to tragedy "as the Greeks saw it" – a reaffirmation of the Hegelian right. This new approach shows "a man who is free within the circle of his own situations, who chooses, whether he wishes to do so or not, for everyone else when he chooses for himself." [49, p. 36] Again, the "world's absurdity" drives the discourse. Its context is the Cold War of the 1940ies and 1950ies between democracies and soviet imperialism. Albert Camus considered Sartre's "Marxism an embracing of a tainted partial perspective, a betrayal of individual consciousness in favor of the collective." [7, p. 399] Sartre, on the other hand, accuses Camus of unwillingness to give up his ideological interests. Camus prefers Hebbel instead of Hegel, looking to the Greek experience and its adaptability for his generation's needs. observes that "the tragic age always seems to coincide with an evaluation in which man, consciously or not, frees himself from an older form of civilization and finds that he has broken away from it without having found a new form that satisfied him." [6, p. 179] The author of "Le mythe de Sisyphe" (1943) describes how his contemporaries have turned human intellect, science and history into a new deity, which has now "assumed the mask of destiny." [6, p. 185] The individual, seeking freedom from this new god, is once more "in the ambiguous and contradictory state that can give rise to tragic expression." [6, p. 187] The veterans who fought the battles are left "Outside the Door", to quote the title of Wolfgang Borchert's 1946 anti-war play, which became the theme for the German post-war-generation.

Most of the poetry written about the Second World War considers the landscape of violence "as a space suspended between the past the soldier has left and the future to which he hopes to return." [26, p. 148] It repeats what already had been said after the first war of the century. And it reflects the experience that suffering is not the result of a visitation from Heaven, as in Greek tragedy, but is inflicted by modern man himself.

The expressionist "cry" for the creation of a new human being, which both the extreme left and right had demanded, has not only led to concentration camps and gulags or graves of "unknown soldiers" and dehumanized protagonists, but also to the conscience of a self as an identifiable entity (with a name, a sex, and a set of personal characteristics). Projected against the historical storms between 1905 and 1989 the human *self* appears lost in the desert and ridden by *angst*.

Gerhard Hauptmann's adaptations of Homer's myths during the years of war replaced both, the Bible and Goethe's *Faust* (the prescribed readings in the German soldiers' 1914–1918 before the Russian winter would kill them.) Since ancient times the self existed in "partnership" either with God or with a philosophy that denied or accommodated Him. Within the judeo-christian culture, mankinds original sin was considered to be hybris, or man's belief to be godlike. It is this belief that Unamuno, for example, insists upon, against all arguments to the contrary by reason and logic (*The Tragic Sense of Life*). But "the shock of violence unaccounted for, unseen, unreal, and unreasonable, meant that the self was separated from most doctrines of sufficient reason; it had to make its 'separate peace'." [26, p. 149] All over the non-totalitarian, free world, from Vienna to Los Angeles, Freud's "couches" became the battlefields of the self. The community did not longer ask for a needed social therapy. "Commitment" became a term for a lost value system. And long before "political correctness" was prescribed by an alienated institutionalized democracy the self had already trained itself to avoid contradictions and conflicts of social nature.

2   Let us step back in time for a moment and focus on why the Greek tragic hero had become the unique type the "lost generation" of World War I could relate to. This had sprung from a double perspective: looking back toward the Ancient laws of the gods, and forward to a new community and nation. The tragic hero is not

an ideal character, but that functions as a warning, addressed to the *demos*, the collective chorus, and not to an aristocratic audience. Those basic circumstances of Ancient Greek theatre returned into the minds of the Western theatre reformers in evaluating the theatrical conventions of their time. The military virtues of courage, resourcefulness, magnanimity and the old code of honor in general were again under investigation and finally rejected. German directors like Reinhardt and Jessner aligned their work along the ancient Greek classics' portrayal of the antagonists and the chorus in order to enlighten the citizens of the newly formed Weimar Republic. Reinhardt's *Grosses Schauspielhaus* had a circus arena in a former market hall converted into a huge regular ancient Greek theatre space by the visionary young architect Hans Poelzig. He realized Reinhardt's dream of bridging the gap between actor and audience and making the spectator part of the action. The opening performance of Aeschylus' *Oresteia* was the 20th century first new interpretation of the play. Its success reflected the audience's recognition of their needs for the upcoming democratic society. Fritz Engels, the drama critique of the *Berliner Tageblatt*, wrote in November 1919: "For the first time we were shown the entire trilogy. What was distant beauty eight years ago has become a real experience. A war between the hemispheres is over; Europe has fought with Asia over a whore, a warrior returns home." [10, p. 5] This performance was the first representative action of a new republican consciousness, rendered for a people not yet aware of its importance for the preservation of the newly gained democracy. The appreciation of the theatre of the ancient Greek texts was able to bridge disparate political and aesthetic positions. From Benjamin to Lukasz they approved: "The essence of these great moments is the pure experience of the self" [40, p. 157]. For the performances of ancient Greek dramas during the 1920ies certain theatrical devices became rules of thumb for cutting through the jungle of the arising questions.

Piscator meant to present "plays of active protest, a deliberate *J'accuse*; a reportage and montage; a warning that history is marching on; political satire, morality plays and court trials, were meant to be shocking on purpose." [12, p. 255, quoted] Piscator had Walter Gropius design a flexible theater-in-the-round, his new interpretation of the Ancient theatrical space for his concept of a total theatre, but he never managed to raise the money to actually build it.

The possibility of creating a new humanity through a cultural revolution seemed greatest in Russia, where a bolshevik *coup d'etat* had toppled the young democracy and replaced it with a bloody regime. Leon Trotzky predicted in 1932 that under these circumstances "man will become immeasurably stronger, wiser, and subtler; his body will become more harmonized, his movements more rhythmic, his voice more musical. The forms of life will become dynamically dramatic. The average human type will rise to the heights of an Aristotle, a Goethe, or a Marx. And above this range new peaks will rise." [57, p. 256] The poet Vladimir Mayakovski recited roughly hewn verses that praised the revolution: "Fall into step and prepare to march!/ No time now to talk or trifle./ Silence, you orators!/ the word is yours,/ Comrade Rifle!/ We have lived long enough by laws/ For which Adam and Eve had made the draft./ Stable history's poor old horse!/ Left!/ Left!/ Left!" [42, p. 131] And Vsevelod Meyerhold initiated an "October revolution for the theater" with stylized sets and actors trained in mechanical gestures. He arranged seats freely in his theatre and issued tickets at random to soldiers and workers. But all the artists' and intellectuals' desire to assemble a mass audience and transform it into an integrated community (of followers of an ideology) was doomed to frustration. As so many times during the 20th century, their individual self-expression failed to live up to the goals of their professions. There is a pathetic note in Klee's admission during his 1923 Bauhaus lectures. All that was lacking in the community begun at the Bauhaus, Klee said, was an audience: "We are seeking a people." [32, p. 55]

By reviving *The Oresteia, Oedipus, and Elektra* (in Hofmannsthal's version), Reinhardt showed the viability of poetic drama on the modern stage. He also restored the possibility of portraying a generalized human struggle by depicting representative figures in conflict with cosmic forces in place of the petty domesticity of the naturalistic drama. Reinhardt's 1919 production of *The Oresteia* in "The Theatre of the Five Thousand", as his new building was called, used an open stage and every available contemporary mechanical device. This production stood for the hope that theatrical spaces would contain modern life as once the great *orchestra* had contained the Greek community. Reinhardt borrowed freely from the techniques of the circus and from Chinese and Japanese traditional theatre. It was his avowed intention to free the theatre from the shackles of literature.

The basic experience of the turmoil of the 20th century is that the self cannot be sustained without some viable ethical code, and thus there were many contrived readjustments. The search for a sustaining identity availed itself of archetypal resources. By returning to one's own "emotional memory," the storage of "stories," the conscience of the self discovered thinking as the capacity for intervention as embodied within the dramaturgy of the ancient Greeks. This position wove together the following two elements: the discourse of the body and the discourse of the law. Their intersections occur within the performer, a body, so to speak "in recess", since the performer's space (as well as the spectator's) is an "in-between"-space (between inside and outside), as well as their time is an "in-between" time (between past and future).

To de-naturalize "obtained truths", to challenge what is perceived "natural" (war, for instance), to uncover the confusion and to detect abuses within the community appear to be only too familiar needs of actual society. In order to determine the twists of history and to survive the clashes of civilizations it is not enough to denounce cartoons and acts of violence.

3   Re-visiting ancient Greek tragedy gives form to raw material. Thus it works in a manner similar to that of nature itself. By observing partially realized forms in nature one may anticipate their completion. Access to this process is provided by current history not through the ancient myths, just as it was for the Athenians of the 5th century B.C., who had to resist the Homeric heroes for their community's needs. But the *orchestra* of the past shows things not as they were but as they "were supposed to be"; hence Aristotle's insistence that poetry work by "probability or necessity." In this way "new interpretations" free themselves from accidental and individual elements. As Aristotle points out in the famous distinction between poetry and history in chapter 9 of the *Poetics*, "Poetry therefore is more philosophical and more significant than history, for poetry is more concerned with the universal, and history more with the individual." [15, p. 17]

By removing the copies of the myths from their truth ancient theatre achieved its creative social performance within the ancient Greek community. In providing a positive function for *mimesis* it taught the revelation of reality, aside from raising moral and ethical questions. In essence, it is the realization of the ideal member of democracy, that is significant for any kind of re-visiting, or re-reading, or re-interpreting the dynamics between protagonist and chorus for the training of a modest law-abiding citizen through rejection of the reactionary nature of the inhumane Homeric hero. "Unhappy the land where heroes are needed", thus Brecht's Galileo defends himself after recanting his doctrine of the motion of the earth. In order to deal with the forces of the inquisition, the KGB or the Gestapo your mind must be free of myths, otherwise there will never be an age of reason as

Euripides, Calderon or Brecht imagined it for the future of their contemporaries.

All interpretations of ancient Greek theatre have focused on questions like these: What is the moral effect of war on human beings? What virtues and vices does it encourage as contrasted with those encouraged by peace? In that manner the modern Western theatre learned not to cast moral judgment on their heroes but rather on the nature of their own existence. It is within this context where the definition of "gestus" becomes the clearest and fullest source of theatrical wisdom to be found within Brecht's writings. For whom does it claim to be of use? What practical action corresponds to it? Ancient Greek theatre was not just about reinforcing the existing social structure and celebrating Athenian democracy. It was also a theatre for raising questions. Athenian society was full of contradictions and the community was aware of the fact, that the future could neither be predicted nor controlled. To check and to balance divergent interests and to find compromises for the whole was a need for progress. The plays call the community to account for its actions and charge individuals with taking responsibility for their decisions. As protagonists struggle toward self-knowledge, their view is frequently distorted by arrogance and passion. Wisdom is achieved only through catastrophic suffering as both tragedy and history has taught us.

4   Let us remember two other basic guidelines Aristotle gives for interpretations.

The *Poetics* Chapter 6, sums up previous thoughts in the central definition of tragedy as "an imitation of a noble and complete action, having the proper magnitude; it employs language that has been artistically enhanced by each of the kinds of linguistic adornment, applied separately in the various parts of the play; it is presented in dramatic, not narrative form, and achieves, through the representation of pitiable and fearful incidents, the catharsis of such pitiable and fearful incidents." [15, p. 11]

From theatre history we know, that the calculated outcome from *catharsis* has proved most troublesome in this definition. Since hundred of years interpretations have grown from different views of tragedy as a whole, but all agree upon *catharsis* as a beneficial, uplifting experience, whether psychological, moral , intellectual, or some combination of these. Last but not least it is a refutation of Plato's charge that art is morally harmful.

Another chapter of the *Poetics* too, the 13th, gives rise to much debate: the description of the preferred hero of tragedy. The *ethnos* (character) is defined as "a person who is neither perfect in virtue and justice nor one who fall into misfortune through vice and depravity: but rather, one who succumbs through some miscalculation." [15, p. 22] But that is beyond any reality of theatre making. It reminds us of our fundamental being. We are man of the city of God and the city of man.

It is not so much that the *self* needs a God, but that it can not stand alone. "It is a comfort to know that patterns of behavior, actual or imagined, are repetitious, shared archetypically with the entire history of the race, are actually a part of a 'collective unconscious', to which each self may attend if the need occurs. This is not to defeat death but to gain a kind of immortality in the sharing of the undying patterns." [26, p. 150] It reflects not just tragic, but common sense of life, asking in changing times for new interpretations.

5   In Chagall's *Time is a River without Banks* the timeless clock, though referring to eternity, may not refer to death. On a broad river floats a tiny boat, apparently a symbol of human life carried on the back of the stream of time. Two lovers lie on the river's border. They are outside of time's stream, oblivious of the passing hours. "To the fortunate time stands still..." says Schiller in *Wallenstein*. This is symbolized by the large pendulum clock without hands which floats in the center of the painting. Above it flies a winged fish which plays the violin. He, like the lovers, has escaped from the confirming streams of time – his music endowing him with wings: the artist lives forever through his art. But his *self* is only of interest, if he participates with his work in the community's competition for defining its narratives.

No doubt, the modern self tries to reread the past in terms of its present situation.

Revivals of Ancient Greek texts "emphasize the heroic struggle with evil, or seize upon dramatizations of force in the near or remote past" [26, p. 149] as productions of Peter Stein and Andre Serban were famous for. The new role the chorus got assigned to was to show, how the modern *self* became susceptible to harm and pain. [20, p. 19–30]

The European mind these days is occupied by the process of European unification, based on the impact of the 1989 revolution in Middle and Eastern Europe and the challenges of the worldwide globalization. But it was the liberation of the *self* in the former soviet occupied nations that re-affirmed a value system, which rejects the former Western policy of appeasement, developed during the division of the continent, and its contempt to dismiss religion. A revived concern about "commitment and community" gives life to newly established democratic institutions and government policies.

What we can learn from re-visiting the Ancient Greek tragedies is that *ethos* is always directly connected to *mythos*. The emphasis is not upon particularizing the character, as in much modern theatre, but upon developing an agent appropriate to the action. It is after all the tragic sense of life we are left with as society.

32 Generality is the Enemy of Children's Theatre*

I am not a specialist for "children's theatre", and as actor and director I have my doubts, if we do need "specialists" for the different groups of our audience. In my experience the most natural situation theatre can have is a "mixed" audience — young and old, male and female, rich and poor — in short: people from all social strata, who attend together a performance. But saying this, I do not question all the great innovations of the last century, like Natalia Sats' Moscow Children's Theatre, founded in 1921, Berlin's Gripps Theater, a result of the '68 cultural revolt, or Launder's Company in Philadelphia, just a few years old. The dozens of such theatres worldwide, who brought a wide range of theatrical heritage – from puppet plays to opera – into the children's mind, are an asset to the theatre world, adults should care for and the society should make accessible to as many children as possible. But most of the theatre people come only occasionally with a pure children's audience in contact. The routine of the majority of Western theatre companies to produce each year for small children and their parents a play, mostly during the pre-Christmas- time, is the usual opportunity for young actors and directors to improve their tools and goals — and to experiment. I am sure that most of my Cypriot colleagues agree, how much we enjoyed playing or directing this shows. Like most other German directors I had my first directing job in a children's fairy tale (Grimm's *Misses Holle*), soon I wrote a "Manifest for a new Children's Theatre", influenced by Brecht's aesthetic, which in the 1960ies in the East German province was still not accepted by the official realism doctrine. Under such conditions the performances for children gave space for experimenting with

---

*First published in Greek in [21].

94

mime, mask, design, music. The exploitation of fantasy was something I gained from my work for children. Storytelling as basic tool of dramaturgy disciplined my intellectual lust for interpretation. I remember that I went into two kindergarten asking the kids to draw event by event the story of one play, using the sketches for the visual narration. (*The Brave Tailor*)

I have no doubt, that the legends and fairy tails of a culture too belong more than anything else to children's upbringing. And the challenges of every day life, of learning, of school, of being human are a playground of a children's audience more than adults can imagine.

What makes performances for children different is that they remind theatre of its roots and down to earth heritage.

First of all it is their sense of truth, of simplicity, and their feelings of wonder and reverence — all of which we need to possess, if we want to re-vitalize theatre. Children remind us, that we too started out as audience members. But what were the things, that draw us to the theatre again and again? What creates those moments that every audience member has had of sitting up in his chair because something struck him in the guts? These moments are under no one person's control, their creation is shared in equally by audience, actor, director, designer, and technician. It is the active participation of a children's audience in the story telling of a performance, which reminds us theatre people, what our job truly is: to act.

For children's eyes an action must be physically capable of being done. Brecht's Social Gestus for example is a functioning relation for them, often observed in the world of adults, already a survival technique in communication, which they are learning, but not yet intellectually defined and for ideological or political interests valued as by their parents. For example, "pleading for help" is something they can imagine immediately. The contradiction between attitude and words is their field of expertise. On the other hand "pursuing the American dream" or "expressing the new socialist human being" is something neither the actor nor the spectator can pick up and can do at a moment's notice. Children as spectators insist, that an action must be something that the actor can actually accomplish onstage.

A next reminder kids bring us in the performance is, that an action must be fun to do. By fun I do not necessarily mean something that makes us laugh, but something that is truly compelling to the actor. Children appeal to the actor's sense of play. Language is a main tool here. The more vital, active, and gutsy the actor's language is, the more life will he bring to the stage because his action will that much more exciting to him and his young audience.

And children insist more than adults that an action must be specific. Already Stanislavsky said, "Generality is the enemy of all art", and nothing could be truer.

To play for children is like acting training. We know, the specificity of an action such as "extracting a crucial answer" will bring an actor to life much more than the vagueness of "finding out something". Furthermore, a specific action will provide you with a clear, specific path to follow when playing the scene.

VI Observations

The demonstrator in the theatre, the actor, must employ a technique by means of which he can render the tone of the person demonstrated with a certain reserve, with a certain distance (allowing the spectator to say: "now he's getting excited, its no use, too late, at last, " etc.). In short the actor must remain a demonstrator. He must render the person demonstrated as a different person. He must not leave out of his presentation the "he did this, he said that." He must not let himself be completely transformed into the person demonstrated.

(Bertolt Brecht, The Epic Theatre [3])

33 Contradictions & Conversions: Dramaturging Mother Courage and Her Children in the United States and Germany, Winter 1994–Summer 1995*

by Kathleen Mary Doyle

As I am squished into a 12×12m holding cell, the electrified gates slam, bouncing their crowning glory, halos of barbed wire. Agitated whispers of "Entschuldigen Sie" are exchanged around me as I politely but stubbornly pry my notebook out from the armpit of the man in front of me. "Gehenze" is bellowed into my ear. I twist my neck to see a friend of mine who is not only acting as if I weren't doing the very same thing with her only last night, but as if she is devoid of a heart and the coursing blood required to pump it. One gets the feeling, however, that she would revive immediately if her own mother would dare to disobey orders and step out of line. The metamorphosis of the American actors into robotic, fascist warriors is complete. Then: just as the crowd's subconscious terror has congealed, we hear calculated, foreboding footsteps on the roof over our heads.

*Part of the performance documentation. Excerpts first published in [9, pp. 23–29]. Reprinted with permission.

A recruiting officer made up with fuchsia eyelids and a white skull dejectedly exclaims:

"How can anybody get a company together in a place like this?" contemptuously glaring right through us. A Puerto Rican sergeant, with vacuous camaraderie, dismally moans: "Peace is a mess!" He goes on to unnerve the forlorn officer by confiding, "I have been in places where they hadn't seen a war in seventy years! Those people didn't know who they were." This line particularly teases the audience, for they too have not seen a declared world war in fifty years and are in the midst of reveling in that accomplishment. Our two military representatives try to convince us that war is essential to establish morality and civilize humanity. Peace, not war is hopeless. And life, without a constant, ominous threat of destruction is absurd. Played at its face value, this scene could have easily been reduced to the four-minute prologue of Mother Courage and Her Children. Instead, it has been milked for all it is worth. At first, converted into a seventeen minute sequence that took place within the audience at the Hawthorne Theatre in Delaware, the irony of the text was addressed to the potentially out-of-reach spectators with accusatory lines such as: "In peacetime, everybody eats whatever they want." Converted a second time to suit, the nerve-wracking confines of a legitimate detention center, however, the potent dialogue laid the foundation for an entire evening of didactic yet entertaining theatre.

Celebrating the fiftieth anniversary of the end of the Second World War, this production, is dedicated to the German-American friendship that has developed over the past five decades. A former American cruise missile station, PYDNA in Hasselbach, has been transformed into an artistic playing space, illustrating the new era of hope, which began November 11, 1989. As recently as two years ago, the presence of this base instilled fear into the hearts of thousands, yet simultaneously provided the surrounding Rheinland-Pfalz area with economic ease. At a national Brecht symposium sponsored by the University of Delaware in February 1995, director Heinz-Uwe Haus looked forward to this spring's remounting of Mother Courage and Her Children in. Germany: "PYDNA has five security bunkers where each door is one and a half meters deep, solid steel. We'll have concrete runway stretching to meet barbed wire caves. To get the most out of our circumstances, we'll find imaginative ways to narrate the story. First, the audience will go from station to station for each scene, like a medieval drama. The second half of the show, we'll let them sit down in chairs, so they'll have the strength to clap their hands at the end." The rocket bunkers, barbed wire fences and asphalt roads create an ideal setting in which to narrate Brecht's message on humans' inability to profit from war.

Demystifying the legend of the Thirty Years War as a religious pursuit, Haus focuses on Bertolt Brecht's belief that war is merely "a continuation of business by other means" that makes "human virtues fatal to those who exercise them." (Courage-model, 1949). Obediently following Courage and her wagon, the audience represents "the little guys" willingly buried in the avalanche of capitalist war debris. The audience becomes bitterly cold and physically fatigued from this production's demands. They may speculate at what point they may be allowed, as a group or individually, to exercise any tree will without the expressionless brigade aborting their attempts and shoving them back into line. In its Cold War heyday, PYDNA generously employed thousands of Germans with the caveat that they and their families would be among the first to die in case of attack by or on the former USSR. The author cannot help but think of Matt Groening's animated characters who aspire to work at "Springfield Nuclear Power Plant" due to its competitive salaries, knowing full well that besides total annihilation, they risk growing a third eye or hair on the palms of their hands. The Hasselbach audience was largely composed or former PYDNA employees. By analogy, it seems an achievement in itself to produce a play that promoted "Homer Simpson" to attend the theatre.

Nearly fifty years ago, in an attempt to defend the "Free World" against communism, steel bunkers were erected upon lush, rolling hills of daisies and herbs, bulldozers blasted through lilac fields, underground hideouts tunneled through rabbit holes, and gasoline pumps polluted frog ponds. Today, with the unification of Germany and the normalization of Europe, US troops no longer occupy the base. Wildflowers wreathe the bunkers' rooftops, sparrows nest in the watchtowers and wild boars wander through the gates that nominally separated the residents of Hasselbach from nuclear destruction. In order to cope with the irrevocable desecration of the once pure landscape, the company decided that a rite of conversion, both natural and artificial, must be performed. Thus in July of 1994, eleven months before the production would begin rehearsal, British painter Glyn Hughes was commissioned to begin work on a project that would include twenty-three gigantic murals. The murals were to be done on industrial canvas and then hung, so as not to incite comparisons to the communal art parade on the Berlin Wall. These paintings were meant to bridge the gap between PYDNA's atomic architecture and miraculous nature. Also, the paintings would serve as the "subconscious storyboard" of *Mother Courage and Her Children*, replacing the typical projected headlines to each scene. Visually, the artwork condensed Brecht's storyline. Hughes' oeuvre often competed with the actors for center stage. Such competition prompted performers to test their limits in rehearsal. After all, Haus encouraged the troupe to "go overboard" with Epic acting until they could "hear Stella Adler rolling over in her grave." The P.T.T.P. could no longer rely on the simplicity of white silk backdrops upon which to project their silhouettes.

As dramaturgy, I collaborated with Hughes and Haus in autumn of 1994, noting specific lines and images from the text that might spark Hughes' imagination. Brecht's text proved a rich source of metaphors: "This milk is good," "Peace is a pain in the ass," "Roses blooming, the balmy air perfuming," and "The stone begins to speak." Hughes' primary job was to translate these literary metaphors into visual metaphors. Designer and director were not opposed to discussing mythical and literary references that might coincide with Brecht's theme of the individual's struggle against history. Despite our perusal of history, however, we made a great effort to remain grounded in the play script and to avoid projecting our personal abstractions.

Hughes' aim was to excavate the submerged fear of, and sense of proximity to, war with which the audience is burdened. In other words, instructed Haus: "He's got to rub salt in the wound."

Hughes also wanted to extend the play's meaning beyond the Seventeenth Century and the life of the characters. Haus and Hughes have collaborated on Brecht productions longer than the author has lived. Their relationship is a deep and amicable one. "I'm always available because it is an extension of my own obsession," says the artist. And, although their interpretations of the text and paintings occasionally collided, each maintained sincere respect for the other's "obsession."

I had the pleasure of assisting Hughes for the first ten days at Hasselbach before the rest of the company arrived. Stranded on an abandoned missile station, free from ordinary distractions like telephones and fax machines and the usual conveniences of heat and running water, Hughes and I met daily to chart our technical and creative progress. We constantly adapted the forms to the surroundings, a challenge that Hughes found particularly invigorating. We also adjusted the paintings' placement on a daily basis. For example, when ruthless winds and torrential rain shredded seven of the hanging paintings, we patched them up, re-painted areas and devised alternatives to hanging certain works.

"Carion" (5×50m) was laid on the side of a hill, hidden from the audience during Scene 12. Each evening thirty-citronella torches illuminated the thirty eclectic, expressionist victims of war, merging the Thirty Years War with the Cold War. Psychedelic pregnant housewives, man-eating ostriches, and naked bodies that have been patiently scratched to death dangle from barbed wire nooses and mustard seed garlands. The feet of the hanged grip portraits of there past lives; including Chaolithic fertility symbols and scavenging tortoises. The portraits symbolize the perpetuation of war upon an already ravaged landscape. "We want to see the dichotomy between the stillness of death and the action of war," insists Haus. This particular painting became a group effort and was the last one completed. Hughes invited the company's curiosity and willingness to experiment in painting as well as acting. On the evening of strike, Hughes cut the "mural" into thirty pieces, giving each member of the cast and crew a slice.

"Pile" (75×10m), which formerly hung from the lookout tower, was exiled to the ground in the holding cell that had first captured the audience. Now the crowd was tree to trapeze through the gates but had to trample over a stack of burnt Brueghel-esque figures. These were the British colorists' imagined corpses, demons and remains from centuries of "civilized" warfare.

As we were reminded not to take Mother Nature for granted, so we wished to remind the audience not to take Mother Courage for granted. The play was in a state of conversion from an indoor to an outdoor production. Actors needed to be cooperative and flexible. Yet the basic *gestus* developed at the University of Delaware stuck. Actors were not to portray "characters" but were to constantly seek unexpected reactions in unexpected circumstances. Because of this "deliberate spontaneity" onlookers were prevented from forming an opinion of a person until the sum of the person's social deviations had been calculated. Actors were indoctrinated in the Brecht legacy: "Don't blot out contradictions in behavior, make them obvious!" Specifically emphasized was each individual's choices in given circumstances. Audience members were not allowed to become indifferent to characters that continually broke the molds.

Preconceptions are challenged as Yvette seduces an elderly, lecherous colonel out of his fortune in order to save Swiss Cheese's life. Instead of delivering the bribe to the executioners, however, she transforms from a panting "900 number girl with the brains of a scallop" to a cunning "hyena" lunging to take inventory of the belt buckles and shirts that now belong to her.

The actress keeps the audience suspended between sympathy and disgust for the heartbroken, camp follower by making her both admirable and repulsive. Audience members, ideally, must constantly reassess their preconceived notions of the dramatis personae and rationally confront their own biases. Realism or Naturalism accepted without reflection actually impedes our vision, so that we cannot face reality. In a sense we are promoting Cubist acting, or performance that deconstructs reality so that all sides may be seen simultaneously.

Rigorous cuts in the script obviated the indispensability of *gestus* in performing Epic dramas. In order to ease comprehension of the predominantly non-English speaking audience as well as to facilitate the endurance required to withstand Hasselbach's inclement weather throughout scenes that lasted up to thirty minutes, omissions of dialogue were dramaturgically justified. Stripping the text of its intellectual satire, we stressed "visual narration." For example, in Scene Three, as Courage anxiously awaits the outcome of her honest son's interrogation, her rumination: "They're not wolves. They're human anti out for money. Bribe taking in humans is the same as mercy in God. It's our only hope. As long as people take bribes, you'll have mild sentences and even the innocent will get off once in a while," is transformed into a physical admonishment of Kattrin: "Scour those knives!" Haus acknowledged Brecht's contention that it is pointless to utter weighted poetry to undetermined listeners. Effectively rendering the text's universal themes more accessible to his audience, Haus actually honored the dead playwright by butchering his fifty-six year-old scripts.

Mother Courage and Her Children maybe Brecht's most structurally boring play. Before the mincing of the text, the title character had more lines than the verbose Prince of Denmark. And distribution of text was heavily imbalanced. "Since I found the play so undemocratic, my primary goal was to find a trick that would make the entire company essential in telling the story."

The company discovered the pregnancy of the headlines. Usually these episodic summaries are reduced to projected super titles that deprive viewers of suspense. Loosed from the noose of sentimentality, viewers can pragmatically criticize the various situations and behaviors exhibited. "In these headlines, we found a basic *gestus* for the play and, without trying, a chorus developed through improvisation. These satyr-plays ended up inspiring us in scene work. We managed to have some pretty heavy scenes between the scenes," says Haus. A case in point is:

Delaware's Scene Nine opens with two men dragging a corpse on-stage and blandly announcing, "Throughout 1635, Mother Courage and her daughter Kattrin pull the wagon over the roads of central Germany." The cadaver adds "in the wake of the increasingly bedraggled armies." What follows is startling: an actress appears in the middle of the audience singing "The Song of The Rosebushes" as Kattrin and her mother become transfixed by the singer's enviable coziness. In Germany, all headlines, announced in the native language, were preceded by the screech of a drill sergeant's whistle and conversely, "The Song of The Rosebushes" is performed on a lush, cadmium yellow hill behind the seated crowd. In the distant horizon, Courage and Kattrin limp along with the wagon for 100 meters until stopping short to catch the final line, "It bore such lovely flowers."

The American production's "chorus" resembled an ancient Greek chorus in more than just their rhythmic stomping and unison movement. They maintained a basic attitude, socially confronting and accusing the onlookers of committing war atrocities for the duration of the three-hour production. This concept was only fortified overseas. The invented chorus became a regiment of automaton-like soldiers, corralling the herd from scene to scene, creating a new episode each time they did so. Shouts of "Vorwärts!" interrupted the beat of silence that had previously concluded each scene. These soldiers were just fluent enough to shame a camera-wielding tourist into submissively snapping his shot from behind the painted white boundary line that separated audience from actors. With perfect rigidity, the chorus blazed through the eerie landscape alternately chanting Brecht's hymn "Our food is swill, our pants all patches. The higher-ups steal half our pay," and the classic "Onward Christian Soldiers, marching as to war, with the cross of Jesus going on before." They unabashedly mocked the Nazi goose-step and trudged down soaking hills in darkness.

The remounting of *Mother Courage and Her Children* had to be elastic, considering the different viewing habits and societal networks of the American and German audiences. The American audience was composed of local subscribers, faculty and students, although some Brecht enthusiasts came from as far as Chicago and Los Angeles. The public was warm and receptive if somewhat removed from the apocalyptic urgency of the anti-war drama. The actors used the entire theatre space and built no barriers between the audience and themselves.

Hasselbach's audience was largely composed of the former peace activists who had lobbied for ten years to shut down the base and who had erected ninety-seven crosses on the outskirts of the gates, one for each missile the base had held. Just twenty-four months ago, this site harbored missiles that within eight minutes of detonation could demolish entire countries in the former USSR. "No Nukes" graffiti became so thick on the wall (200×6m) that it had to be blasted off. Significantly, after three performances, the same walls were decorated with peace dove stencils and slogans including "We're in this together" and "Support Mother Courage."

Like troopers themselves, audience members endured 10C temperatures, rain and two hundred breeds of mosquitoes. Equipped with umbrellas and blankets, Germans celebrated theatre's triumph over nuclear armament by enthusiastically following Mother Courage and her notorious wagon from bunker to bunker. The last four scenes were staged in a barren pit at the center of the base and began around 22:00h, just as the sun was setting. Characters' voices echoed through the security bunkers and the regiments' close order drills cast monstrous shadows across the missile silos.

Brecht wanted to rub our noses in the contradictions in our everyday life. His aspirations should not be reduced to one socio-historical or ethno-cultural peculiarity. "You gotta hit them where it hurts." quips Haus. Each production came up with original *Verfremdungseffekts*. The most striking example was invented in the United States. Immediately after Mother Courage lullabies her dead daughter "to sleep," she viciously blames the peasant couple for killing her child. Such shocks keep the audience guessing. Courage stoically unfolds an army blanket to cover Kattrin's body when, suddenly dollar signs appear in her eyes. Seized by greed, she scavenges the corpse right down to the skivvies. The sight of the actress, nearly naked, lying in a puddle stunned the Germans. Whenever I sat in the stands, I heard the gasps. This was our *gestic* conversion of Brecht's merchant-mother conflict.

Dramaturging for Haus, my primary task was finding the "events" within the episodes and then finding the "contradictions" within these events. When extreme contradictions were not apparent we implanted them. A microscopic scene-by-scene analysis precluded all imaginative inventions, however. "Stay grounded in the text" and "Look until you find the hidden contradiction," he hounded me. Each event needed its own *gestus*. Ours was a "basic aggressively which was nearly vulgar." "Our audience will have to be a bit masochistic," jokes Haus. Epic Theatre demands these behavioral contradictions to balance its didactic message and complimentary perspective.

Brecht docs not delve into character relationships to understand an event. Potentially emotional scenes, like the executions of Eilif and Swiss cheese, take place offstage as in ancient Greek tragedy. Also, after the emotionally charged action occurs, the scene typically halts abruptly. The playwright is not interested in showing the emotional effect of death on the loved ones. Instead, one scene ends and the next begin, often set years later in another country. Little or no mention is made of the previous trauma. Epic narration in Mother Courage and Her Children represents an historical process, depicting human inventiveness required to survive through a war. At times the literal context of the dramatic events, in this case the Thirty Years War, proved inaccessible to contemporary American actors. So we came up with metaphors for events.

Just as Brecht does not always create chronologically consistent headlines, we did not feel obligated to logically sustain a metaphor in order to string events together. Rather, a myriad of metaphors were noted. Haus encouraged using metaphors to relate pedantic themes to his "corn-fed" actors. These synthetic implants are designed to bring out offensive physicalizations of Brecht's text.

The conversion from the indoor black box theatre to a sprawling, outdoor performance art piece fostered a curious experimentation. For example, in Scene Two, a bunker's steel doors part to reveal the Swedish General, the Chaplain and a beaming Eilif. The general is enthroned atop one of the few pieces of furniture employed. Acoustically these barracks are alive. The line: "Because what you did (mass murder) was in the service of God, that's what counts with me," reverberates with a Darth Vader quality. In Scene Three, Yvette's tent is an old latrine fifty meters away from Courage's camp. The actress had to run back and forth in her bare feet or spike heels through thorn bushes and briar. "The Song of Fraternization" is pantomimed on the station with erotic vogueing on an army not-safe-for-drinking-water faucet. In Scene Four, Mother Courage stages her sit-in outside an actual commander's former headquarters. The James Dean "wannabe" enters by trampling over the general's forget-me-nots. Crucial lines are spat in German like "Leck mich am Arsch!" At Hasselbach, just as Courage told the sentry "I've changed my mind. No complaint," a fall-out siren sounds and a bunker's door lowers. Courage and her chorus of bodyguards charge down the illuminated missile bed.

Over the course of dramaturging *Mother Courage and Her Children*, from Delaware to Hasselbach, I discovered that despite all his theories, Brecht is not really prescriptive. He believed in changing alienation effects to explicitly disturb the audience to whom he was directing the production. The initial academic process of devising alterations necessary to refit our production to suit new, foreign circumstances snowballed into a liberating, collaborative effort. This is what makes doing Brecht fun, deliberately upsetting the audiences' expectations by deviating from the established norm with dramaturgically justifiable, practical quirkiness.

Even if that means that Mother Courage's inner monologue at the last moment of the play becomes "I always hated those brats anyway!"

34 Literary Metaphors into visual metaphors – Experiences Working on Threepenny Opera*

by Glyn Hughes

Throughout all the "scenic illustrations" there is a deliberate change of style. Some only refer to the subject. Maybe one line is extended into the main image. It would be pointless to "explain" the whole lyric, for then, the visual would merely be a repeat of the verbal as in a first book for children, e.g., under an *orange* is the word *orange*.

Brecht's lyrics are much, much more complex. Not only do they push the narrative and help the audience to consider the situations in the play; they enable both the actor and audience reconsider meanings. To emphasize or to stress a line, maybe, or even part of a line — audiences' thoughts may take flight.

It's a play on-the-go. Nothing is static — even the pauses. All the many levels could need this extra visual persuasion. And, hopefully, even succeed in bringing all the strands of consideration and emotion together for a moment of theatre in which all the audience can cohere.

In what is titled as "A Little Song Polly Gives Her Parents to Understand That She Has Married Bandit Macheath," the image is seemingly of a bollard, a rope, a river (or sea), and what could be a boat. However, the bollard is most definitely a phallic symbol while the boat could be a pinned down female sexual organ, although the pins-nails could be paddles of a moving boat. *Snap* goes the rope. The colors are strong too: two shades of red, green, and intense blue. The image by nature is static. Caught after a moment of Polly saying: "and as he'd no idea of treating a girl with due respect I could not tell him: No."

The "No They Can't Song" (Mr., Mrs. Peachum) kept up for Macheath and Polly on their stolen bed. Why? To strengthen the gestus of the situation. "The actor has to tell the spectator more about his character 'than lies in the part'. He must naturally adopt the attitude which allows the episode to develop easily. At

---

*The notes are an excerpt from the dramaturgical material for the production of the play by the PTTP, University of Delaware, Hartshorn Theatre, Newark, opening performance March 11, 1999.

Glyn Hughes, Welsh painter, living in Nicosia, Cyprus, created a "visual fable", which became part of the stage design by William Browning.

the same time, he must also set up relationships with episodes other than those of the story, not just be the story's servant … Polly is not only Macheath's beloved but also Peachum's daughter. Her relations with the spectator must embrace her criticisms of the accepted notions concerning bandits' women and shopkeepers' daughters." (Brecht)

Let's have a look to the "Wedding Song of the Less Well Off", is offers the most ambiguous image in the play. It is interesting to note that even in the original sketches of the forms they can be taken as brutally sexual or spring like. EROS as destructiveness or delicate blooming.

"The Ballad of Immoral Earnings" (near "Insecurity of Human Condition") Botticelli and the Archaic. Instead of Venus (Aphrodite) arriving by sea foam on a shell, we have the pimp (Macheath) in a classical pose (nude), surrounded by broken archaic figurines of women.

"Second Three Penny Finale: What Keeps Mankind Alive!" We do not want to ignore the fact that millions are daily tortured, stifled, punished, silenced, and oppressed. As Weill says: "If the operatic framework cannot stand such a comparison with the theatre of the times [Zeittheater], then that framework had better been broken up." The song has more than one metaphor, of course. In this particular visual the "erotic-low-life" is let out. The director's aim is to show gestures that are to speak the habits and usage of the body. WORK is humiliating—the face with prisoner's cage teeth at the top of the picture frame is the oppressive power. The drudge is implied by boots weighting up the spinal-road of a worker. This image could easily be transferred to "The Cannon Song". This, of course, would not do for modern warfare or, indeed, deliberate unemployment.

"Insecurity of Human Condition" [First Finale (still up during the brothel scene and its image)]. This image jumps further away from the literary metaphor but still keeps the gist of the story.

> *The world is poor, and man's a shit*
> *We should aim high instead of low*
> *But our conditions such this can't be so.*

We jump from the slums of the East End of London (an area where many immigrants came from Europe at the time) to the present. The upturned legs tied to a "body-case" floating in space belongs to the army of sweatshop workers.

The continuity and the conditioning is of the present day although, of course, Colonial repression was certainly rampant during Queen Victoria's reign. Now, of course, it goes under AID and that AID, too, is misused.

Although the original images were drawn in Nicosia, they were enlarged in the Newark workshops. Haus and Browning also reallocated the order for stage positioning of the hangings. This application of imagery (an extended story line) reached considerable dramatic power. This was especially so in the last two songs: the "Ballad in Which Macheath Begs All Men for Forgiveness" and the "Third Three Penny Finale — Appearance of the Deus Ex Machina."

The Ballad has the image near the stage-place of execution (back-stage-right), but The Finale image is shown at extreme back-stage-left. This image is of strangulation and the opposite of the STAGE FINALE. As Brecht says: "The mounted messenger guarantees you a truly undisturbed appreciation of even the most intolerable conditions." When golden drapes drop down from the flies; as do lit chandeliers, in comes regalia dressed Tiger Brown, Deus Ex Machina. The Finale strangled image is still tucked behind, but seen during the dead serious chorus at the end as Brecht requests it to be sung and acted. And here the cockney accents of an earlier London are replaced by Contemporary American. Nos haec novimus esse nihil. "After all, if a judicial murder is to be shown, there is surely no better way of paying due tribute to the theatre's role in bourgeois society than to have the journalist who establishes the murdered man's innocence towed into court by a swan." (Brecht)

35 Notes on Heinz-Uwe Haus Rehearsing Brecht's The Life of Galileo*

by Richard A. Davison

In a staged play the words and actions need to be painstakingly integrated. Selection of the proper cast can be crucial. In rehearsal great attention must be

---

*Richard A. Davison, Professor Emeritus of English, University of Delaware, presented his observations from rehearsals at the III. Brecht-Symposium of the University of Delaware, 3. March, 2007, on the occasion of the opening of *Life of Galileo* by Bertolt Brecht, produced by the Professional Theatre Training Program, UD, Hartshorn Theatre, Newark; his paper has been published in [8]. Reprinted with permission.

paid to the actor's physical appearance, vocal intonations, physical positioning, movements, gestures, along with the set, lighting, sound, props, costumes.

Attention must be paid to detail. Directors (and actors) can learn a lot from skilled writers. They would do well to consider the advice of writers whose works also depend on great attention to detail.

Listen to Lorraine Hansberry on *A Raisin in the Sun*:

> "I believe that one of the soundest ideas in dramatic writing is that in order to be universal you must pay great attention to the specifics." [53, p. 283]

Listen to F. Scott Fitzgerald's opening sentence of *The Rich Boy*:

> "Begin with an individual and before you know it you have created a type; begin with a type, and you find you have created — nothing." [11, p. 317]

Listen to Hemingway's sage advice to a young writer:

> Watch what happens today. If we get into a fish see exactly what it is that everyone does. If you get a kick out of it while he is jumping remember back until you see exactly what the action was that gave you the emotion. Whether it was the rising of the line from the water and the way it tightened like a fiddle string until drops started from it, or the way he smashed and threw water when he jumped. Remember what the noises were and what was said. Find what gave you the emotion; what the action was that gave you the excitement. Then write it down making it clear so the reader will see it too and have the same feeling that you had. ...
>
> When people talk listen completely. Don't be thinking what you're going to say. Most people never listen. Nor do they observe. You should be able to go into a room and when you come out know everything that you saw there and not only that. If that room gave you any feeling you should know exactly what it was that gave you that feeling. Try that for practice. When you're in town stand outside the theatre and see how the people differ in the way they get out of taxis and motor cars. There are a thousand ways to practice. And always think of other people. [24, pp. 219–220]

In his new book *Notes on Directing* [22], Heinz-Uwe Haus writes:

> "The actor must develop his faculties in the art of observing human relationships in everyday life, as well as investigating what may lie behind the society in which the relations occur." [22, p. 8]

The results of these observations must be expressed on stage in specific, concrete terms. Without specifics, theories remain impotent.

Add to this a remark by Brecht that dramaturg Christopher de Haan quoted in the program for the 1998 Yale Repertory Theatre production of *Galileo*:

> "If the critics would view my theatre as spectators do without first emphasizing my theories, then what they would see would be simply theatre, I hope, of imagination, fun and intelligence."

Brecht's demand that we not lose our reasoning power in the theatre does not mean we cannot have a good time, fun. It does not mean we will not be deeply moved by his work.

In memory I am still moved by the two separated lovers in the 1992 Professional Theatre Training Program (University of Delaware) production of *The Caucasian Chalk Circle*, jumping joyfully up and down on opposite sides of a river of artificially lighted billowing silk cloths shaken by actors. At the same time that my mind was aware of the "non realistic" river and the often ironic consequences of human choices, my heart went out to the lovers. My mind explored the ironic consequences of complicated political and social choices made by us and for us that can lead to disaster. The mind was working but so were the emotions. The lovers' permanent separation still breaks my heart. But the over-all effect did not turn off my mind. Good theatre (Brechtian or otherwise) grabs us both emotionally and intellectually.

Actors in a play are ultimately not just talking to each other — they are talking to us. To quote from Notes on Directing once more, "Theatricality focuses on the tension between the actor and the audience." [22, p. 6]

Much has been said about Brecht's theories. I would like to focus on the engine that drives them — on the skills of the director who brings to life the words on the page. Here are some illustrations of the stagecraft I observed at the rehearsals of

Galileo. First, Professor Haus worked with a well-cast group of actors who, under his guidance, became a harmonious ensemble. (I recall the 2002 star-studded New York production of *Arturo Ui* – headed by Al Pacino – which failed not for lack of talent but for want of ensemble unity.) The PTTP actors learned how to work together within the story of *Galileo* from the past and at the same time establish a rapport with the audience in the present.

Professor Haus worked closely with the set and lighting designer (William Browning), costume designer (Andrea Barrier), choreographer (Joann Browning), music director (Linda Henderson), voice coach (Deena Burke), stage manager (Brian Vincent Griffith), carpenters, prop people, et al., and with each actor in regard to even the smallest details that served the whole. Throughout the month or so of rehearsals that I frequently attended, he welcomed suggestions from all. He always recognized what would work best on stage, starting with the simple set: a large stationary platform on each end of the stage and two large moveable staircases that back-to-back formed a third narrow platform. Haus and William Browning agree that, in Browning's words, "If any scenic element is not essential it is probably in the way." [5, p. 52]

On opening night (and, of course, in subsequent performances) Haus's attention to detail – from the small stone to the huge banner – was realized in a coherent and powerful production.

Let me now focus on Professor Haus's running comments to the actors, calculated to engage the audience in Brecht's world. First, a scattering of his comments, then those regarding the scene featuring the Pope.

Always with that eye for detail and balance and impact, Haus would adjust a chair or a prop ("always FIVE books on the table, one in Latin"); he would point or gesture regarding the location and spacing of the actors and the furniture, the timing of the vocal and physical movement:

To Galileo, in reference to the Little Monk's struggle with his commitment to the old faith or the new science: "You have the fish — tell him he is a mathematician not a priest."

To the Little Monk (when Galileo puts the scientific papers on the stair): "The hungry bird snaps them up and reads them." Reason wins.

To the whole cast regarding the choral chanting of a key passage: "To make it clearer clap between key phrases, clap with the cups of the hands." "Don't be too loud. Keep the dogs on the leash." "Bite the words: Oak Tree, not oaktree."

"It is not about scholarly achievement or progress. It's about social implications."

"The Church is responsible to the people of the country, the Campagna."

The very old reactionary cardinal "should move like a 595-year-old tree — no blood — the only thing that works is the brain — ice cold, old and smart."

To the betrayer: "You walk out with five tails between your legs."

To Andrea in his last scene with Galileo: "That was very nice — the walk — that arrogant walk — that sailor walk before you stand with your hand on the top side of the platform. You give your answer in your walking. You go from a nod at the beginning of the scene to a bow at the end. The audience will get it."

Regarding preserving the peasants' faith in the Ptolemaic view of the universe: "What destroys faith is evoking men's faith. It's a kind of wisdom. If you don't touch a vase it won't break. If you touch it, it might break. Leave well enough alone."

In the recantation scene Galileo's three assistants have been told that when the bells of St. Mark's ring at five, Galileo will have recanted. As five o'clock approaches they wait, hoping against hope that he has not recanted. In counterpoint Galileo's daughter Virginia is on top of the platform behind and above them, praying that he has saved his soul by recanting. Silence — then a brief respite of their joyous relief before the bells toll. To the assistant Federzoni: "You have to find the right moment when YOU think it's five, and the audience goes with you. This time it was 3/10 of a second early. 'NO!' must go through the body first. Wait for your body to react before 'NO!' In those six seconds before the bells, time seems to stretch forever. When you feel it, you believe it is five o'clock and the bells have not rung because Galileo has not recanted. Then the bells ring."

Before the first complete run-through: "The proof of the pudding is tonight. OK, guys, let's do it. Concentration. And GO!"

Brecht's succinct stage directions set up the scene "The Pope":

> *Room in the Vatican. Pope Urban VIII (formerly Cardinal Barberini) has received the Grand Inquisitor. In the course of the audience he is robed. Outside is the shuffling of many feet.*

Galileo's scientific theories have challenged the authority of the Bible and the Church. The Grand Inquisitor's purpose is to convince the Pope that Galileo must be coerced to recant. The Pope's opening response is "No! No! No!"

Professor Haus had the Pope (Galileo's fellow scientist and friend) stand in profile in a simple white undergarment, on a carpet in the middle of the long stage. He faced the four dressers (in simple white robes) and the Grand Inquisitor (in a red gown with touches of white and a red cap) with his back to the staired platform at the edge of the stage. Faintly audible sound effects signify the shuffling of the Pope's uneasy flock which depends on him for guidance.

As the dressers (through most of the scene) methodically, ritualistically put on the Pope's religious accoutrements, the man, the human being, the fellow scientist and friend of Galileo became, ever so gradually, item by item, the Defender of the Faith. As the man became the Office, the person became the Personage, and Galileo's fate was unalterably sealed. While the Grand Inquisitor made his case, the four dressers, two by two, brought to the Pope, one by one, the symbols of his office: his shoes, cossack, cape, capelet, stole, necklace (papal crucifix), papal ring, hat and staff (crozier), until the Pope stood tall in the grandeur of his miter and layers of rich white brocade.

The Grand Inquisitor does most of the talking, although in this staging virtually no words were needed to dramatize the shift in the balance of power. It had occurred before the tall, elect, fully costumed Pope turned and strode to and up the stairs to the platform, turned again to face the Grand Inquisitor, now far below him, and intoned, "At the very most, he can be shown the instruments!" The Grand Inquisitor deferentially replied, "That will be enough, Your Holiness. Instruments are Mr. Galileo's specialty." With his assent that Galileo must be made to recant (albeit without physical torture), the Pope moved 180 degrees from his initial refusal: "No! No! No!"

The scene was brilliantly conceived and executed. Much painstaking preparation went into the powerful tension, the conflict beneath the apparent simplicity of this brief scene. Just the right set and costumes and props and lighting reinforced the Pope's inner struggle — with more than just Galileo's fate in the balance. Just the right sound effects suggested the persistent "shuffling of feet," the outside pressures on the Pope.

During many rehearsals Haus worked with the four dressers on demeanor, carriage, and movement as they slowly adorned the Pope. They worked on timing and precision, keyed to the speech of the Grand Inquisitor and the silence of the Pope. They practiced deferential bowing, hands at sides, and taking off their shoes before stepping on the carpet and putting them on before leaving to gather the next symbolic article. They practiced putting on each item: "Better when you put the cape and cap on from the back." "The end is nice when you come to each corner of the carpet." Haus urged the Grand Inquisitor to "not bully or be loud or menacing." Just speak "calmly and reasonably and Relentlessly." "You are not Mephistopheles or the devil." "With the office of the Pope come certain obligations." "Don't get into a fight." Regarding showing Galileo the instruments: "Don't take the extra step by putting it under [the Pope's] nose." "Show as little emotionalizing as possible — what must be done must be done." "Just give the facts — don't pressure the Pope." "The logic of your argument will win him over."

The above comments just scratch the surface of all that went into the Heinz-Uwe Haus/PTTP production of Galileo to create a productive tension between the actor and the audience. I have not talked about the management of drum and mime, posters and banners, clowns and jugglers, ballad singers and stilt-walkers (who handed out cards with lines from the play such as "Truth is the child of time not authority") or the giant Galileo puppet.

As Professor Haus said to his actors and crew, "The proof of the pudding is tonight." Galileo proved no exception to my happy experiences with his nourishing productions of *The Caucasian Chalk Circle*, *Mother Courage and her Children*, *The Good Person of Szechwan*, *The Three Penny Opera*, and *Arturo Ui*. I dined well at the opening night of *Galileo*.

36 The Risks and Rewards of Diversity: An Actor's Experience in a Staging of Oedipus Rex*

by Charles H. Helmetag

From November 16 to December 4, 1994, German Director, Heinz-Uwe Haus, staged a production of Sophocles' Oedipus Rex at Villanova University, in which I had the pleasure of playing the role of the blind seer Teiresias. Haus is well known in Germany, Greece and the United States for his stagings of Shakespeare, Brecht and the ancient Greek classics. The works of Sophocles, of course, have their

---

*Charles H. Helmetag (Professor of German, Chair, Department of Foreign Languages and Literatures, Villanova University, Pennsylvania) works regularly as actor in the Philadelphia area. The text is part of a longer rehearsal report.

own unique history in the German theater; one need only think of the sensation created by Max Reinhardt's virtuoso handling of crowd scenes in his 1910 staging of Oedipus Rex in Berlin and the influence of such classical works on German dramatists. (...) I shall focus my comments on the role of diversity and non-traditional casting in Haus's production, a classical Greek play staged by a German director with an American cast and crew.

The chorus has become a problematical aspect of staging Oedipus Rex in recent years, an archaic device which seems unrealistic or impedes the action. In desperation directors have sometimes let a single actor speak the lines of the chorus or have even dispensed with the chorus entirely. In Haus's production the chorus was not a static narrator or commentator. On the contrary, they became the central character, a dynamic entity which reacted to the turns in the plot and on occasion actively moved the action forward. The chorus represents the people of Thebes and, after all, the king derived his power from the people; that is where the real power resides.

Accordingly, Haus devoted more rehearsal time to the chorus than to any of the principals. Chorus members were encouraged to utilize their own personalities and life experiences, to improvise and to go beyond a realistic interpretation of their roles. Dr. Andrew Tsubaki, a professor of theater and film and East Asian culture at the University of Kansas, provided choreography for the chorus and other cast members. He added an oriental component, including elements of martial arts and the Noh Theater, to an already disparate group of actors. The choreography was intended only as a framework, however, as a guide or suggestion. Basically, Haus trained the chorus members to reach inside themselves for modes of expression. The result of this mix of choreography and improvisation was "kinetically exciting" production.[1]

---

[1] Interestingly, Director John Tillinger achieved something comparable in the recent National Actors Theatre production of *Inherit the Wind* in New York. As described by theater critic Clifford A. Ridley, Tillinger turned the townspeople of the fictional town of Hillsboro, Tennessee (a twentieth-century *polis*, if you will) into "a truly rowdy crowd, heckling the defense and cheering the prosecution. Although some of this is in the script, Tillinger takes it a large step further by assigning the spectators a number of clearly audible adlibs that punctuate the courtroom arguments and the speechifying ... in the (courthouse) square. This ... gives the crowd a set of human faces rather than a single, monochromatic one." [48, p. 6] Some sixteen months before Tillinger's production of *Inherit the Wind*, Haus, through his concept of diversity, succeeded in giving "a set of human faces" to the chorus of Sophocles' Oedipus Rex.

As dramaturg, the director selected a young graduate student known to the cast as an experienced costume designer who had just played an eleven-year-old girl in James Lapine's *Twelve Dreams*. Now Haus was not only relying on her for research assistance but also entrusting her with the responsibility of editing and abridging one of the world's greatest and best-known dramas. She cut at least fifteen pages from the original text, reducing a choral ode, for example, from forty lines to five lines. Interestingly, such abridgement – along with the highly physicalized performance of the chorus – served to heighten rather than weaken the impact of the choral odes.

The speeches of the chorus were sharply reduced in length, but their words gained new meaning because of the "action" context in which they were spoken, because of the physicality of the performance of the chorus members. In keeping with this emphasis upon visual, physical performance, props were kept to a minimum, lighting was unobtrusive and the set was simple: little more than two huge, stark wooden doors. Both the plague and the oracle were suggested by a huge, white parachute silk, a prop utilized by Haus in his two American stagings of Brecht's *Caucasian Chalk Circle*.

Primitive musical accompaniment, appropriate for the Thebans, whom Haus described as barbarian, was provided on drums by a professional musician, an African American, and a seventy-year-old woman, a student of Native American Indian culture, who played Native American drums and shook rattles made of bones and sea shells. These two musicians were visible to the audience at all times. Haus decided at that outset, that only hand percussion instruments should be used. The drums were played with hands, fingers and palms, never with drumsticks or mallets. In addition to the Native American drums, congas, bongos and African talking drums were used quite prominently. Various rhythms were employed to reflect the action on stage. Different types of drums in turn permitted a variety of pitches. Low pitched drums in a slow tempo reflected death or the plague while the high pitched bongs with fast, light, earthy rhythms accompanied a celebration. The musicians and their instruments derived from African and Native American culture not only created a unique sound and atmosphere but also brought an added dimension of diversity to the production.

The Villanova University Theater Department encourages "a flexible, imaginative and non-traditional casting policy," which involves the casting of ethnic minorities or females in roles where race, ethnicity, or sex is not germane. Several

years ago (ca. 1981), for example, a woman was cast in the role of the Salvation
Army Officer, Arvide Abernathy in a production of *Guys and Dolls*, making her
Sarah Brown's aunt instead of her grandfather,--and African American actors have
sometimes been cast in roles written for Caucasian actors. A young African American played Harry the Horse in the above-mentioned production of *Guys and Dolls*
(and was given Nicely-Nicely's song "Sit Down You're Rockin' the Boat"), but, interestingly enough, this practice has particularly been observed in plays by Bertolt
Brecht. In 1985 an African American actor played Peachum in *The Threepenny
Opera*. In the 1970s an African American played Shen Te in *The Good Woman
of Setzuan* and scenes of the North Philadelphia ghetto were projected onto the
backdrop to relate the setting of the play to the audience's contemporary reality.
And in 1980, when Haus was a guest director at Villanova, he cast an African
American in the role of Grusha in *The Caucasian Chalk Circle* to underscore the
fact that she was not the biological mother of the noble child. In the 1994 staging
of *Oedipus Rex*, however, Haus employed non-traditional casting more radically
and consistently than in any other Villanova production that I have scene or heard
of in the past thirty years.

There was an element of risk involved when Haus chose young graduate students as his lighting designer and dramaturg, but he (Haus) took a major risk
by casting the most disparate group of actors he could find: nine men and eight
women ranging in age from 18 to 70 (including a karate expert, a balloon sculptor
and a former nun), graduate students in Theatre and members of Actors Equity
with years of professional experience along with people who had never performed
publicly before. The roles of Oedipus, Creon and Jocasta were played by graduate
theater students, two of them members of Actors Equity. A professional musician
— an African American — provided primitive accompaniment on native drums.
Certainly it would have been easier for Haus to start with a group of experienced
actors, indeed actors with experience in the chorus of a Greek tragedy, but he
intentionally selected the most varied company available.

I, myself, was a special case in that I had never been in a play at Villanova before
although I had performed in a number of campus and community productions
elsewhere. There was an element of risk involved for me to display anger in public
in the role of Teiresias. A very close friend from another academic department
said that he couldn't imagine me as an "angry old man." In fact, the director had
to constantly remind me in the early rehearsals to discard any innate congeniality

and deliver my lines "sharper."

The members of the chorus — graduate theater students, undergraduates and members of the local community — had to take even greater risks. Lovely young women had to put on drab, formless sweat suit-like outfits and floor-length woolen coats which weighed ten pounds each. They had to apply ugly gray makeup and wear grotesque, dwarf-like masks. Their hair was concealed under babushka-like "doo-rags." They also risked physical danger as they ran, danced and jumped around a fairly confined stage area which was a modified (3/4) theater in the round measuring approximately 4 by 6 meters (11.5' by 20') along with athletic six-foot-tall male actors.

Haus advised the chorus members at the outset: "Throw out your personal ambitions of wanting to look good and just put everything you've got into it." This philosophy led to frequently exuberant, almost intoxicated performances on the part of the chorus, especially in the choric odes. Haus's use of the ancient Greek technique of using masks to permit the actors to "get in touch with" their bodies, to experience and use them differently and more fully in performance, could be the subject of a separate paper. As you know, Bertolt Brecht borrowed this technique in some of his productions.

"Through intricate sounds and movement, the chorus developed the setting, reflected the cultural milieu, commented on the action, guided the audience responses and interacted with the play's principal characters through Choragos, the chorus leader." Choragos was played by the theater department's public relations director, and Actors Equity candidate with extensive stage experience, but a person who is more likely to get results through gentle persuasion (or nagging) than by exerting her will. She is a fairly petite woman in her forties, the mother of seven children, who characterized her role under Haus's direction as the first time she was required to "risk totally." Her casting in this pivotal role caused one professor at the university to comment: "She's a very nice lady, but I can't image her bringing up the forcefulness and leadership skills required of the chorus leader." The risks both she and Haus took in this bit of casting paid off. She acquitted herself admirably, her voice became stronger and (as required) more trenchant with each performance, in something akin to a Brechtian double perspective she came across simultaneously as a distinct character and still part of the chorus ensemble, and her performance received special mention in at least one or two reviews.

This element of double perspective or complementary perspective was an important element in Haus's conception of the chorus. The other chorus members were six men — four graduate students in theater — one of them a high school Drama/English teacher with stage and film experience, and two undergraduates, one of them known on campus for his entertainment making balloons at parties and other social events, — and six women — a college freshman with a black belt in karate who turned eighteen during the run of the play, an African American graduate student and a secretary at the University (both of whom had experience in dance), a recent Villanova graduate who is a member of Actor's Equity, a young investment advisor, and a 70-year-old graduate student in Theater who had been a professional storyteller after spending thirty years as a cloistered nun.

How does a director handle such a diverse group? Will they be able to cooperate? Will the individuals with extensive acting experience resent the novices or vice versa? Well, there was definitely tension during rehearsals and several performances in the relationship between one actress and most of the other chorus members. However, they all seemed to surmount the strained relationship for the good of the production.

Haus stated in an interview that he wished to present the story of Oedipus as a visual event and a social event. Therefore, it was necessary to make the chorus the focus of the action, since at the time of Sophocles the audience was the chorus and vice versa. Like Brecht and Shakespeare, Sophocles made use of a complementary double perspective in which the chorus members were both narrators of and participants in the action. In Haus's staging, the chorus members occasionally sat down on benches immediately in front of the first row of audience seats so that the demarcation between actors and audience became blurred as it were, so that the chorus made the audience feel a part of the action, an extension of the Theban community, and thus the chorus seemed to join the audience in reflecting public opinion.

Ironically, the Thebans turn to Oedipus, their trusted leader to save them from the curse and plague which have been put upon their land. This introduces another important element of the play: the political dimension, the effect which the actions of political leaders have upon the lives of their constituents. In rehearsals Haus frequently compared the situation of Oedipus — and his subjects — to that of contemporary political figures: to Gorbachev, Reagan, Nixon, even to local political leaders in the small township in which Villanova University is located. In looking at Oedipus, he was more intrigued, for example, by the effect of a president's resignation and humiliation on the American people than by the private ordeal of the man, Richard Nixon.

From the beginning of rehearsals, Haus told the cast members to look at news programs on television and to read the newspapers and new magazines to find parallels between the situations in the play and current historical events. Coincidentally, the 1994 elections took place in the course of the run of the production. One Philadelphia newspaper reported: "Millions of Americans rose up last Tuesday ... cast out Democrats and voted in Republicans." And the headline read: "Voters send messages, but what message? Their anger made history, where it leads is less clear." The article went on to say: "Although the opening line of the chant is clear, it starts to break into discordant choruses beyond that." The newspaper was reporting on American politics, but at the same time it perfectly described the situation of Oedipus and the reactions of the chorus, the polis, to this situation — even in theatrical terms of anger, chanting and discord.

I remember Uwe saying once, "Art is not about symmetry." The chorus members represented widely different ethnic, racial, geographic, religious, cultural, educational and experimental backgrounds in keeping with Haus's conception that the chorus should represent all levels of Theban society, American society and humankind. (In effect, he gave Sophocles' chorus a "set of human faces.") He took this group of people with the most varied cultural, intellectual, religious and life experiences and different levels of theatrical experience and challenged them to take risks, to "embody the narrative" and to make choices which affected his production. The diverse personalities necessarily had an impact on the way the events were projected to the audience. Such diversity enriched the drama with fresh viewpoints (24) as each member of the chorus dealt with the historical events from his or her own personal perspective. All of these players had to accept their colleagues' differences and develop a sense of complete confidence in each other. Only then could they hope to achieve the effects which the director wanted to achieve. The chorus found its identity as an ensemble by experiencing, tolerating and accepting the diversity of its members and each individual's unique contribution.

37 Music of the Spheres: Singing Actors in The Life of Galileo*

by Linda Henderson

I have had the privilege of working with Uwe as music director of *Mother Courage*, *Threepenny Opera*, and most recently, *The Life of Galileo*. The actors of PTTP are not trained singers, but because of their fine sense of vocal communication, we were able to incorporate the music written by Hanns Eisler into our production.

The musical score arrived last summer, and so began the puzzle of translation and matching songs to scenes. Since the text of the score is all in German, I used a combination of the verses in the script, which is translated by John Willet, and word-by-word translation.

The score calls for the voices of women and children, as well as a balladsinger. Three actresses sang the soprano, mezzo, and alto lines for most of the production, and a tenor took the role of the balladsinger.

Hanns Eisler scored the play for flute, clarinet, and cembalo. We adapted to the musical colors at our disposal, always with an awareness of the celestial bodies described in the play. First, not having access to a harpsichord (cembalo), I experimented with various kinds of thumbtacks, finally deciding on metal tacks stuck into the hammers of an upright piano. The result was brilliance when I played forte, and a delicacy when the notes were played lightly, like a harpsichord or clavichord. The general sound of the ensemble was glittery, an appropriate reflection of the stars. We positioned the instruments at one end of the stage area, visible to the audience and sometimes part of the action. Since there was no amplification, the balance between the instruments and voices was a constant consideration, but the orchestration was such that the instruments never overpowered the singers.

Three women were chosen to sing the introductions to each scene, and we drew upon their abilities to color vocal production between head and chest voice, as well as their exceptionally good sense of pitch and intonation. They sometimes

---

*Linda Henderson, Adjunct Professor, University of the Arts, Philadelphia, is a concert pianist. Her text is an excerpt from a report published in [25] about experiences as music director of *Life of Galileo* by Bertolt Brecht, a production of the PTTP, University of Delaware, opening March 3, 2007, Hartshorn Theatre, Newark. Reprinted with permission.

mimicked the sound of a boys' choir, sometimes brayed like fishwives, sometimes sounded like angels.

An unusual aspect of our production was the inclusion of a narrator who played djembe, an African drum similar to a conga. This actor punctuated the beginning of each scene with either a single stroke or a roll followed by the announcement or banner which precedes each scene.

Our production opened with an ensemble prologue, an exposition of "the Earth 'round the Sun business" involving the entire cast. This ensemble invited the audience in to the story rather than merely letting them observe. The cast members handed out small pieces of paper with slogans on them, some of Galileo's words. During this section, we encouraged the actors to use a "second talent" beyond acting, such as juggling, gymnastics, walking on stilts, and playing the harmonica. The point was to have them play an attitude, which was separate from the characters they would later play. Led by a rhythmic cadence supplied by the narrator, the cast cartwheeled, somersaulted, and juggled onto the stage. The narrator set up a rock and roll rhythm to the chant, "The Sun stands still, the Earth is on the move." The first singing began during the prologue, with a female actor who would become the balladsinger's wife. Dressed as a gypsy, she belted out an unaccompanied bawdy tune comparing her marriage and fidelity to the old ideas concerning the Earth's prominence in the universe. We drew the lyrics and melody from scene ten, the carnival scene, as well as the next part, an actor exhorting the giant puppet of Galileo to stop putting ideas of self-worth into peoples' heads. The balladsinger then took over, presenting the opening lines to song number one, "In the year sixteen hundred and nine, science's light began to shine."

The three women, using their "angelic" voices, sang song number one. The audience is reminded of the crystal spheres that Galileo would soon shatter. The first soprano holds high F as she sings, "The Sun stands still," while the mezzo and alto answer with "the Earth is on the move." The song was presented with beautiful tone but in a dispassionate way, merely announcing the sphere-shattering event. The beauty of the harmonies played against this serious announcement.

All the songs functioned as scene change music. Sometimes the women moved set pieces as they sang, or stood still in different places around the set. We performed the play in a long, relatively narrow space, with audience in bleacher seats on two sides. The actors therefore had more choice of physical placement than if we had used a proscenium stage.

Song number two opens with a flute cadenza over an A♭ major chord, a calm that lasts only four measures before tumbling into a rhythmic allegretto section. The trio sings in unison, in a lower tessitura, conversationally explaining to the audience "Even a great man must practice some deceit."

Many of the songs mention the date of the action to come in the following scene, keeping the quality of the songs as lessons. Song number three describes Galileo's realization that "there is no Heaven," a phrase sung beautifully by the trio, followed by another brief flute cadenza, but ending this time with a crashing d minor chord from the piano. It sounds as though things are starting to fall apart in the universe. This d minor chord has a little dissonance, a B♭ clashes with the D-F-A of the chord, making it more jarring. I find Eisler's harmonic vocabulary to be fairly predictable, not nearly as dissonant as Paul Dessau's setting of *Mother Courage*, for example, but there are edgy sections which make a statement, like this one. That extra B♭ hints at ominous things to come.

We did not use song number four, "Quaedam miracula", until the end of the play as a musical finale, and used song number four variante instead to precede scene four. Again, the women sing in unison, a melodic line based on sol mi la, a quote of the childhood taunting tune, and an alienation effect. These words are, "The old way says, as it now is, it ever shall be. The new way says, if it's no good, goodbye!" The word "goodbye" is a tri-tone, and dissonant chords accompany the song. The scene that follows reflects the frustration set up by this music, when the Grand Duke of Florence and his advisors refuse to look through the telescope.

Song number five is similar musically to song number two, but the words are not snide comments about Galileo this time. The women report that the chief astronomer, Clavius, has upheld Galileo's findings, and the listeners feel relief hearing this, especially with familiar music.

At this point in the play, Uwe made some changes. In our production, song number five preceded the scene labeled six in the script, and we cut the scene labeled five, the one concerning the plague. Likewise, the scene labeled seven became our scene six. This scene contained more music than any other. It opens with the women, in harmony and with much melisma, singing of Galileo as a guest in Cardinal Bellarmin's palace. The florid lines nearly obscure the bite of the lyrics, which tell that the Inquisition has begun to stifle Galileo.

We gave this scene some background music, an idea taken from the Berliner Ensemble's 1979 production. The delicately played tack piano became the sound of a harpsichord at the party, and I improvised a G major minuet in early Baroque style, followed by a rigaudon as the party progressed. However, as the two cardinals began to threaten Galileo, a darker g minor minuet accompanied the action. Interspersed with this music was a G major diatonic harmonica, played by one of our actors portraying a musician at the party. There is also an offstage madrigal sung by the women's trio, telling that "this lovely springtime cannot last." As in the 1979 production, I used music from the original finale by Eisler.

The final scene of Act I was originally scene ten, the carnival scene. It, like the prologue, involves the ensemble, where the only recognizable characters are the balladsinger and his wife. He tells the audience about the dangers of an educated public, giving several examples of lower classes rising to challenge authority. The song is by far the longest in the play, and we added the balladsinger's wife for several of the examples. The whole ensemble sang the chorale at the end of the song, encouraging people to "kick out the bosses and fire the pastors." The action of the play is stopped here as the actors once again engage the audience directly. At this point in the play, the ideas of Galileo are part of the public consciousness, and so must be illustrated by the common folk.

Act II opens with song number seven preceding scene eight, the scene with Galileo and the little monk. The three women sing in unison, a brisk, business-like announcement of the scene.

We chose song number eight variante to open scene nine, an elegant waltz sung in three-part harmony, another example of the music playing against the threat described in the action.

The scene with the Pope opens with clangorous chords and a wild descending scale from the piano, followed by a gruff melody presented fugally by the flute and clarinet, leading up to the women's exclamation of "The Pope!" During this scene, our cast imitated the sound of shuffling humanity that was irritating Barberini as he became Pope. We used breath sounds and soft striking and rubbing of the railings behind the audience to achieve this background noise. It was appropriately irritating to both the Pope and the audience.

Scene eleven is preceded musically by a steady allegretto, rhythmically relentless, as though what is about to come is inevitable. It is the scene during which Galileo recants, sung cheerfully by the women. The lyrics are, "It was a day in June, 1633, a day of infamy for you and me. When the age of reason was so near, for one whole day science had no fear." As the scene progressed, the women stood in the audience and sang out the part of the bells of St. Mary's, tolling out the news of Galileo's recantation. As Galileo entered, they sang to a tune heard earlier, "the Earth is on the move!" I chose the tune of song number four variante, the one built on a diminished triad. As the women sang this wrenching melody, two very large pieces of fabric were ripped from the walls behind the audience. The fabric had quotes from the play on them, Galileo's new ideas, and the ripping sound punctuated the song. Immediately, though, the action stopped, the lights changed, and the ensemble assembled to recite the entire discorsi. The attitude was one of reassurance, that even though Galileo recanted, the truth was out and could not be put back. The entire cast was involved, even the actors playing the Pope, the Cardinal Inquisitor, and Galileo. By alternating between specific characters and anonymous chorus, the actors told the story in two different ways. Much of the discorsi was recited in unison, but some lines were recited solo, some words were elongated, pulsed in a soulful way, and some lines were sung.

We finished our production with the scene at Galileo's house in the country, where the church imprisoned him until he died. The melody before the scene is the loveliest in the play, with the potential to elicit sympathy from the audience. It ends, however, with the words, "'til the day he died," as a repeated rising perfect fourth, reminiscent of another childhood taunt, and another example of the alienation effect. The women sang it without emotion, simply stating that this was where Galileo spent his final days. Since we cut the final scene, we decided not to use the finale from the score, which includes references to the scene at the border. Instead, we used an earlier cut piece, song number four, "Quaedam miracula." The ensemble sang in two parts, a rousing canon in, G major, leaving the audience with a hint of optimism.

VII Appendix

> Vladimir: *Ah yes, the two thieves. Do you remember the story?*
> Estragon: *No.*
> Vladimir: *Shall I tell it to you?*
> Estragon: *No.*
> Vladimir: *It'll pass the time* (PAUSE) *Two thieves, crucified at the same time as our Saviour. One —*
> Estragon: *Our what?*
> Vladimir: *Our Saviour. Two thieves. One is supposed to have been saved and the other...* (HE SEARCHES FOR THE CONTRARY OF SAVED)... *damned.*
> Estragon: *Saved from what?*
> Vladimir: *Hell.*
> Estragon: *I'm going.* (HE DOES NOT MOVE.)

(Beckett, Waiting for Godot [1, p. 12])

38 Visualizing Space, Actions and Events – Example of a Pantomimic Dramatization

Max Reinhard: *The Miracle*
  SCENE I ... CATHEDRAL

Characters

The Nun	The Lame Piper
The Abbess	The Knight
The Old Sacristan	The Madonna

127

Nuns and Novices, Peasants, Townsfolk and Children. Bishops, Priests, Monks and Pilgrims, Cripples, Blind, Lame and Lepers. Patricians of the Town, Knights and Troops of Soldiers.

1. The interior of an early Gothic Church.

2. High, massive columns rise into mystic darkness.

3. Gothic arches, stone ornaments representing tendrils and lace work, a richly decorated iron grating, entangled scrolls and figures.

4. Narrow, high church windows in deep, rich coloring.

5. Aisles, corridors, doors, an unsymmetrical arrangement of mysterious openings, windows, stairways.

6. Votive statues on columns, small statues with candles and flowers before them, crucifixes, offerings brought by grateful people, wax flowers, embroideries, jewels, a child's doll, decoratively painted candles.

7. In the background a richly carved altar, with a golden shrine and candles seen through a grilled screen.

8. The eternal lamp burns before it.

9. A Cardinal's hat hangs above.

10. Alter, with table, to divide and open, with steps through it.

11. The floor is of large gray stones, some of which are tombstones. In the center of the floor the stones are to be glass with lamps below, so wired as to spread the light from the middle outwards.

12. Flickering light from behind columns as from invisible candles throws fantastic shadows.

13. Shafts of sunlight, coming through the high windows at the right, project patterns on the floor.

14. At left and right of auditorium [stage directions read "right" and "left" from the point of view of the audience], cloisters with vaulted ceilings and stone floors.

15. Chandeliers of various sized in the auditorium to cast light downwards only, adding depth and mystery to the ceiling.

16. Several poles for flags and lanterns fastened to the seat ends in aisles of auditorium.

17. Panelling of balcony rail to show here and there between flags.

18. A clock above pulpit. This clock is to strike at various times during the dream parts, to suggest the existence of the church. Remember the sound before the clock strikes.

19. On top of the clock two figures to mark the hours, by striking a large bell between them. One of these figures symbolizes life; the other death.

20. Clerestory windows around upper part of auditorium. Choir stands and triforium openings below windows.

21. All doors have heavy bolts, locks and knockers to create business and noise.

22. Large keys on rings for various doors.

23. The doors immediately behind proscenium lead to sacristy.

24. The doors below the loges lead to exterior.

25. Small midnight Mass bell, near top of tower, to be rung from rope on stage floor.

26. Wind machines, thunder drums and voices also to be there.

27. When audience take their seats, everything is dark.

28. The sound of a storm far away.

29. Soft candlelight in the auditorium, only where it is absolutely necessary, and flickering behind the columns around the alter screen.

30. Clusters of candlelights in distant places in the auditorium and stage high up in the tower to produce an effect of tremendous size and of incredible distance.

31. There are to be candles around the altar itself. The candles should be of various lengths and the bulbs of very low voltage and of various pale colors.

32. In chapels tiny candles suggest side-altars against darkness. Prominent clusters of them unsymmetrically chosen. Flickering candles on the columns in the apse and cloisters throwing shadows.

33. Candles on altar, altar screen and in chapels to be wired individually and lighted or extinguished by nuns. Candle bulbs to be no larger than one-half inch in diameter. The bulb must not show.

34. Candle extinguishers and wax tapers.

35. The large altar is dark.

36. One recognizes gradually among the towering columns several dark figures huddles together absorbed in prayer.

37. From a distant tower a bell sounds.

38. Large bells are located in ventilating shaft over auditorium and controlled from orchestra gallery.

39. A praying voice from behind the triforium windows is indistinctly heard; now and then a Latin word is audible.

40. Chairs are pushed about, some one blows his nose, other cough. The echo resounds through the church.

41. After that, silence.

42. An old sexton appears carrying a lantern.

43. His stick taps the pavement, and his steps drag over the stone floor.

44. He pulls back the green curtain over the Madonna statue.

45. He goes to the tower. Up the winding staircase the lantern shows through little windows and finally at the top.

46. He crosses a bridge and disappears through a doorway in the wall.

47. The organ starts and bells ring high above the church.

48. Nuns in pairs march through the cloisters toward the alter in two long columns, to take part in the coming ceremony.

49. The windows of the church become more brilliant from sunlight without.

50. Out side a young bright spring morning has awakened.

51. Sixty nuns dressed in ivory-colored garments trimmed with black. They all wear ropes. The black nuns' costumes appear like shadows passing in the dark and must be cut in such a way that the white undergarments show conspicuously when the nuns flutter like white doves in their excitement at the loss of the Madonna.

52. The chin cloths must be drawn very tightly, so that they never look slovenly. In fact they are to be made so that they can not be worn otherwise.

53. On e column is headed by the Abbess.

54. The Abbess may be dressed wither in white or in black, wears a crown and carries a silver staff, like the Bishop's, but smaller.

55. In this column the aged feeble Sacristan of the convent is carried in on a chair by four nuns.

56. In the other column a young nun, still but a child, is led in. She takes a tearful farewell to her mother, father, and grandmother who are seated at the right.

57. In an impressive ceremony the young Nun is dressed in an over-garment similar to that of the old Sacristan and received the keys and office.

58. The Abbess sits in a special chair during the ceremony. She sings while one nun holds a music book for her and another holds a lighted candle.

59. This is accompanied by responses without music from the choir gallery.

60. In front are the holy pictures and the statue of the Madonna which stands on a column. It is a stone statue, painted in blue tempera and gold-leaf and wearing a crown set with precious stones

61. The statue is to look as stonelike as possible and heavy, even if clumsy.

62. She must wear the white muslin nun's garb, as an undergarment.

63. The white head-cloth always has to remain on and be drawn as tightly as possible.

64. The Madonna holds the child in her arms.

65. The pedestal is decorated with many flowers, and large and small candles.

66. Crutches stacked around the base.

67. This pedestal altar conceals steps, covered with soft rubber. There must be supports for the Madonna under her armpits, at her waist, a seat, and recesses cut in floor for her feet. Her shoes are rubber-soled.

68. There are five statues of saints at other positions.

69. Large bells in the distance begin to sound as the Convent Church is revealed in its full glow of light.

70. The Nun, for the first time as the new Sacristan, opens all the doors with her keys.

71. A great commotion and the hum of voices come from without.

72. The sound of music grows nearer, the organ starts with massive tones

73. A great procession pours into the church through all the doors. Men and women who are making the pilgrimage to the celebrated miracle-working statue of the Madonna.

74. First come the visiting orders of nuns in white.

75. Then peasants with banners.

76. Women in vivid-colored clothes, some barefooted.

77. Townspeople following, carrying banners with coats of arms of towns.

78. Tradesmen carrying the various emblems of their trade on poles.

79. A group of peasants bring in an enormous cross.

80. A great crowd of children with a Maypole.

81. Priests carrying church banners.

82. Acolytes swinging incense.

83. Choirboys with their large books.

84. The Archbishop carries his staff and walks beneath a canopy carried by four men.

85. Under another canopy is carried the monstrance. Church dignitaries follow.

86. Then monks carrying wooden statues of saints on poles.

87. A great mass of cripples on primitive crutches and stretchers, wearing dirty ragged clothes.

88. Blind people, who are led.

89. Widows in mourning.

90. Mothers carrying sick children on their backs, in their arms, and with other clinging to their skirts.

91. Lepers with clappers.

92. Pilgrims with broad-brimmed hats, staves, bundles and flasks.

93. Finally the knights in vivid color.

94. Followed by heralds, squires, men-at-arms, in full dress.

95. No one comes empty-handed. All who have nothing else to carry bring full-leafed birch branches.

96. The procession fills the whole stage and all the aisles in the auditorium.

97. There is much singing and waving of the yellow green branches. It looks almost like a green forest, waving to and fro.

98. The voice of a priest, whom on one sees, is heard.

99. The music stops.

100. A bell rings at the altar.

101. A white vapor begins to rise from the vessels containing the incense.

102. The crowd falls on its knees.

103. The sick crowd up to the statue of the Madonna and pray without halt. The Archbishop leads the prayers from the pulpit.

104. The tension grows. A breathless silence.

105. Finally there arises in the audience a completely lamed man, who had been carried in on a stretcher. He gets heavily to his feet, with convulsive twitching, and raising his arms high in ecstasy strides to the figure of the Mother of God, where he dances with joy.

106. A cry, the organ, rejoicing of the crowd. A miracle has come to pass.

107. The pilgrims leave the church singing.

108. The candles are extinguished and the nuns slowly pass out.

109. The young Sacristan goes about her duties of locking the doors.

110. In the last doorway there stands the healed fellow blowing harmlessly upon a flute. This demoniac figure, who runs through the play and has an evil influence upon the fate of the young Nun, is the lure of sensual life. At this moment his appearance resembles that of the Pied Piper. He wears a broad-brimmed hat over his faunlike ears.

111. Children surround him in their curiosity and listen to his music.

112. The Nun stands still as if under a spell and hears his tunes with the same astonishment and naïve joy as the children.

113. The children, unable to resist longer, fall into the rhythm, crowd into the church and force the Nun, who resists, into their ranks.

114. An unconscious yearning for the spring without causes her momentarily to forget her new office.

115. In her childishness, the Nun lets herself be forced into the dance.

116. She lets her keys fall and dances joyfully.

117. In the meantime, the Piper's tune has attracted a young Knight, who quietly enters and is fascinated by the graceful dancing of the Nun.

118. Suddenly, on seeing him, she becomes frightened and rooted to the spot as they exchange glances.

119. The Nun hears nothing as the bell rings fro vespers.

120. Nuns approach in a column, the Abbess at their head.

121. They become enraged on seeing this pair in the church.

122. The children and the Piper slyly escape through the open door.

123. The abbess rebukes the young Sacristan who stares about her, dazed.

124. At a nod from the angry Abbess the keys are taken away from her and the heavy bolts locked behind the Knight who ha slowly gone out.

125. She is sentenced to spend the night in prayer before the statue of the Madonna.

126. The nuns again depart and the church sinks gradually into night and silence.

127. The Nun prays fervently before the statue of the Holy virgin.

128. In her confusion she scarcely knows what is happening to her.

129. Her thoughts, which she seeks vainly to discipline, escape through the stone walls and wander tirelessly into the night in the direction of the young Knight.

130. The poor child returns again and again to her prayers, seeking peace and comfort there.

131. Her youth, awakened for the first time, struggles against the cold discipline offered her.

132. She runs to the font and sprinkles herself madly with holy water.

133. Her heart beats wildly, she throws herself about on the steps leading to the miracle statue.

134. She wrings her hands and plunges desperately into passionate prayer.

135. At this moment something happens that can just as well be a raving dream of fever as a fantastic reality. With the rapid pace of dreams, one experience chases after another and drives the Nun back into the church after a moment of actual happiness through a martyrdom of indescribable suffering. Dream, or reality. It is intense, terrible, vita, as endlessly long as an intense dream, as horribly short as a full life.

136. Suddenly there is a light but insistent knocking at the gate. The Nun grows tense.

137. The knock is repeated. Is it her own heartbeat? She tries not to hear and prays aloud.

138. The knocking continues, always louder, and finally sounds from all sides and from all doors. Each door should have a heavy knocker.

139. She springs up involuntarily, takes several steps toward the door.

140. She stands still in fright, throws herself on her knees, wrings her hands, is torn back and forth.

141. Finally like an excited but caged bird, she flutters anxiously to and fro, beating her head against the cold walls.

142. The knocking grows wilder, her yearning more uncontrollable.

143. She shakes the locked doors with all her strength.

144. Throwing herself on her knees, she begs the Mother of God to set her free.

145. The moon shines through the windows.

146. As if mad, she dashes toward the Holy virgin and points fiercely at the child in her arms. She is yearning for the child, for everything out there.

147. Completely out of her mind she finally takes the holy child from the arms of the Madonna and holds it high.

148. A warm glow radiates from it and then suddenly the child disappears in a flash of light.

149. Everything grows dark. A sound like thunder resounds through the high church.

150. When it is again light Mary has heard the passionate pleadings and has performed a miracle.

151. The high alter glittering with candles, slowly opens, forming a Gothic arch, with a knight in silver armor and a blue mantle, visible through the high candles on the altar tables.

152. The Knight and the Nun stand regarding each other.

153. The Nun shrinks back frightened and flees to the foot of the Madonna.

154. The Mother of God smiles as graciously as ever. Her will is plain.

155. The altar table, with the candles on it, opens slowly, exposing a flight of steps.

156. The Knight slowly approaches the Nun. She rises shyly.

157. He offers her his hand to lead her forth. She looks at her clothing and hesitates to go out in her holy costume.

158. She removes the black nun's veil, the white cape, the rosary with its large cross, the belt and finally her dark dress and lays them all tenderly on the steps of the miracle statue.

159. Rising, she shudders at the sight of her underdress, feeling that she is without clothes.

160. The Piper who was behind the Knight brings in the blue cloak of the Knight and covers the young Nun with the dress of life.

161. Again she kneels, and the Knight with her, at the foot of the Virgin.

162. Then he catches her in his arms and runs off with her into the world.

163. The church is deserted.

164. A sign comes from somewhere within the walls.

165. The Madonna statue begins to glow with an unearthly light.

166. It seems as if she were opening her lips and smiling. The figure moves.

167. The light on her face changes from unearthly to the pink of life.

168. She opens her eyes.

169. She smiles.

170. She turns her head.

171. She drops her robe.

172. She descends.

173. She lifts her arm.

174. She removes her crown.

175. She holds it up high.

176. She lays it on the pedestal.

177. Then she gives a sign for the altar to close, and it becomes as before.

178. The virgin bends low, and in sweet humility puts on the simple costume of the Nun.

179. She goes to the tower and rings the bell.

180. Voices of singing nuns. The Virgin kneels and prays in front of her pedestal.

181. The nuns come into the church for mass.

182. The Abbess glances at the supposed Nun, sunk in prayer, and chuckles fondly at the repentance of her favorite.

183. By accident her glance falls on the spot where the miracle statue has stood, but now where only her cloak and crown lie. She does not trust her eyes, stares, consults the sister.

184. A terrible fear seizes all the nuns.

185. They scream, run around enraged, cry out, weep, threaten their supposed sister, fetch the priest and ring the alarm bell.

186. With clenched fist and swinging cords, all rush at the poor Nun, who has obviously permitted the theft of the precious treasure in her impious sin.

187. The Nun's head remains humbly bowed.

188. Whenever the threatening sisters surround her in a wild rush, she gently floats a short distance into the air without changing her position. This is done on a trap on the right.

189. In silent awe they draw back from her; staring at this miracle speechlessly, they recognize that a higher power is obviously at work here, and that the young Nun is the chosen agent.

190. Returning to the earth, she goes about her duties like an ordinary nun, taking a jar of oil to fill the eternal lamp.

191. The nuns form open rows and follow their holy sister spreading their arms wide and singing in ecstasy.

192. The scene grows dark.

39 Theatre Terms

ABSTRACT SET   An attempt to capture the "idea" or "concept" of a setting without resorting to realistic construction. "Sketches" scenes through the use of drapes and set pieces, such as window and door frames.

ACT   1. To play a role on the stage in front of an audience. 2. The basic division of a play.

ACTING IN QUOTES   The Brechtian concept of acting in which actors comment on the actions of the characters they are playing rather than maintain continuous identification with the character. Demonstrating contradictory behavior of the character.

ACTION   The movement of the actors and the unfolding of a play's events.

ACTOR   The central artist of the theatre who creates a dramatic story on the stage through words and gestures. Frequently the actor expresses the language of a playwright; theatre, however, can exist without playwrights, but it cannot exist without actors.

AD LIB   On-the-spot improvisations — word or gesture — that were not originally in the script or added during rehearsals.

ALIENATION EFFECT   The Brechtian idea of distancing the audience from a performance through breaks in the narrative and the suspense to promote critical awareness. (See Verfremdungseffekt)

ANAGNORISIS   In classical Greek tragedy, the frequently used plot device of "discovery" or "recognition."

ANALYSIS OF THE PLAY   Not an academic, but practical procedure of theatre making. Brecht suggests: Find out what socially valuable insights in impulses the play offers. Boil the story down to half a sheet of paper. Then divide it into separate episodes, establishing the nodal points, i.e. the important events that carry the story a stage further. Then examine the relationship of the episodes, their construction. Think of ways and means to make the story easily narrated and to bring out its social significance.

ANTAGONIST   The character who stands in opposition to the leading character (protagonist) of a play.

APRON   The space on stage in front of the curtain line. Sometimes used interchangeably with forestage.

ARENA STAGE   A form of center staging in which the audience surrounds the stage on all sides. Sometimes called theatre-in-the-round.

ARRAS SETTING   A half-circle of unpainted draperies that serve as a formal background for the stage area.

ASIDE   One of the conventions of theatre in which the audience accepts the idea that the words spoken by an actor, with appropriate side gesture and tone, can be heard by the audience but not by the actors onstage.

AUDITION   The process through which actors seeking roles in a play or positions with a theatre company present monologues or scene readings for a director.

BACKDROP   Large flat area, usually canvas hanging at the rear of the stage, that can be painted to represent the desired locale. Today the backdrop usually represents the sky and is sometimes called the "skydrop."

BACKING   Flats or drops used to mask the backstage area by limiting the audience view through doors, windows, or archways in the set.

BACKSTAGE   The area behind the proscenium arch that, during the production of a play, is not seen by the audience.

BEAT   The basic units of an actor's role defined by changes in character motivation.

BEIJING OPERA   A form of Chinese theatre first introduced in 1790 that relies on music, singing, and acrobatics to express dramas based on the traditional Chinese way of life. Domestic relationships and military conquests were frequently the subjects of Beijing Opera, which also used mythical subjects to reinforce accepted values.

BERLINER ENSEMBLE   Founded by Bertolt Brecht and Helene Weigel in 1949 in East Berlin, following the much acclaimed production of his play *Mother Courage*. Guest performances of the company in Paris 1954 and London 1956 revolutionized Western theatre and soon established his concept of *Epic Theatre* worldwide as alternative to *Socialist Realism* as well as "Aristotelian" tradition. After Brecht's death in 1956 and with the erection of the Berlin Wall in 1961 the theatre came under pressure of the communist government and compromised some of its aesthetics. Since the 1989 revolution the theatre is not any longer a model of Brecht's theatre practice.

BLACK BOX   A flexible theatre space in which the stage space and the configuration of the audience space can be changed from production to production.

BLACKOUT   The sudden extinguishing of the stage (but not house) lights. This is used at the end of an act, or to separate scenes or sketches, or for some special dramatic effect.

BLOCKING   The movements or locations of actors onstage.

BORDER   A short curtain often hung above the stage to mask the flies when the set does not contain a ceiling.

BORDERLIGHTS   A series of lights hung above and toward the front of the stage area to provide general illumination.

BOX SET   The standard set for contemporary realistic theatre, showing a back wall and two side walls, with the fourth wall understood to be the "transparent one" through which the audience views the play.

BROADWAY   The long street that runs through the heart of Manhattan, home to the largest concentration of professional theatres in New York City.

BURLESQUE   A stage exaggeration of a person or object that destroys reality for comic purpose. In terms of entertainment, a format that developed in the United States, featuring comic monologues, skits, and, increasingly, naked girls. Little seen since the 1940's.

CATHARSIS   In classical Greek tragedy, a "purging" of the audience by arousing pity and fear. It is a process whereby the spectator learns to control his emotions.

CHEAT In acting, to turn the body slightly out toward the audience while seeming to play in profile.

CHORUS Originally a group of approximately fifty men who performed songs and dances — dithyrambs — at religious celebrations. Out of these choral dithyrambs grew the classical Greek tragic drama. The Chorus remained as part of the drama but was gradually reduced in size until it became, finally, an onlooker and commentator.

CHRONICLE PLAYS Dramatic versions of stories from such chronicle historians of England as Raphael Holinshed. *(The Tragedy of King Richard the Second)*

CITY DIONYSIA A festival in ancient Athens that became a major event for the presentation of drama. The festival was held in honor of the god Dionysus, who is closely associated with the Greek theatre.

CLAQUE Audience members who are friends or relatives of performers, or hired especially to applaud and cheer loudly, thereby giving the impression of general enthusiasm for a particular actor or performance.

CLASSICAL TRAGEDY Tragic plays written either by Aeschylus, Sophocles, or Euripides. In a limited sense, later plays that follow the model developed by Aristotle.

CLIMAX The moment in a play of the highest dramatic or emotional intensity.

COMEDY A term generally used to describe plays in which the characters undergo embarrassment or discomfiture, and even severe physical accident, but so handled that pain is not present and the audiences are interested and amused without feeling profound sympathy. The action usually turns out well for the major characters. (See also such specific modes of comedy as Romantic, Farce, etc.)

COMEDY OF HUMORS A mode of comedy established by Ben Jonson, which derives from the Medieval concept that the body (and the character) is controlled by four fluids: blood, phlegm, black bile, yellow bile. An oversupply of one or another fluid causes excessive behavior and, thus, comedy. *(Every Man in His Humor)*

COMEDY OF MANNERS Plays dealing with the intrigues and counter-Intrigues of highly sophisticated ladies and gentlemen living in an artificial, polished society.

The comedy grows out of the violations of these artificial social conventions, as well as out of sparkling dialogue and wit. *(The Country Wife)*

COMIC RELIEF Humorous speeches or incidents woven into the fabric of tragedy that are sometimes used to enhance and enrich the action but always exist primarily to relieve tragic tension. (The drunken porter in *Macbeth*.)

COMMEDIA DELL'ARTE A form of street theatre that began in Italy near the beginning of the fifteenth century and spread all over Europe. The players worked improvisationally from scenarios. Such characters as Harlequin and Pierrot, still seen today, grew out of the commedia.

CONSTRUCTIVISM A graphic-arts movement that became popular, especially in Russia, in the early part of the twentieth century. It was adapted to theatrical sets by Meyerhold. The essence of constructivism is to display space as a series of planes furnished with distorted objects.

CONVENTION In theatre, a special relation between the audience and the play, in which the audience accepts certain obvious departures from reality. (Aside, Soliloquy, Monologue, etc.)

CORPUS CHRISTI PLAYS Generic term for the cycle plays of the Middle Ages that were produced on Corpus Christi Day (the Thursday after Trinity Sunday).

COSTUME DESIGNER The theatre artist responsible for interpreting plays through the costumes created for the actors.

COSTUME PARADE In the theater, the first showing of the costumes on the set and under lights for approval by the director.

CROSS-GENDER CASTING The casting of actors of the opposite sex in roles written for either men or women. In many early Theatres, men played the roles of women characters. In recent productions, cross-gender casting has been used as a strategy to explore issues of gender identity.

CUE Anything that causes something to happen. For the actor, it refers to the line or event just before his or her character speaks or moves. It can also refer to a change in the lighting or sound.

CUE-TO-CUE A frustrating form of technical rehearsal in which the actors are asked to jump from light cue to light cue. To be avoided if at all possible or conducted without the actors, since it is disruptive to the actors' experience of the rhythms of the show.

CULTURAL REVOLUTION   The 'cultural upheaval' initiated by Mao Zedong and his wife Jiang Qing in 1966 and executed with mass deportations and killings, with the goal of reforming Chinese society. During the Cultural Revolution traditional forms of theatre were repressed and replaced with model performances that presented an obvious political point of view.

CYCLORAMA   A very large piece of light-colored fabric stretched across the back of the stage that serves to create expansive lighting effects and to silhouette actors.

DEMONSTRATION   Bertolt Brecht's idea that the actor does not "become" the character completely but, rather, "demonstrates" the character's behavior for the audience while still expressing some attitude about it. While this may sound like "indicating," the good Brechtian actor's passionate commitment to the ethical point being made gives the performance its own special kind of reality, whereas ordinary indicating feels merely empty and unreal.

DENOUEMENT   From the French, this means "untying the knot," which is to say, the end of the play, when the last plot problems are resolved or unknotted.

DEUS EX MACHINA   Literally "God from the machine." In classical Greek tragedy a person or dummy suspended from the roof of the stage house to represent the god who would resolve all the problems of the play.

DEUTERAGONIST   The "second actor" of classical Greek tragedy. Often a supporting actor — friend or confidante — to the protagonist.

DIRECTING BOOK (REGIEBUCH)   Invented by the German director Max Reinhardt. Famous is his directing book for *The Miracle*, first time made public in an elaborate commemorative volume published in 1924, during the run of the play at the Century Theater in New York. Since then a basic tool of the directing profession.

DITHYRAMB   In ancient Greece, a choral ode performed by a chorus of approximately fifty men at festivals honoring Dionysus, the god of wine and the reproductive force of life.

DOMESTIC TRAGEDY   Plays with bourgeois or lower-class heroes and heroines who suffer from commonplace trials and tribulations and are usually defeated to provide audiences with a moral exemplum. *(George Barnwell, or the London Merchant)*

DOWNSTAGE   The part of the stage nearest the audience.

DRAMATIC ACTION   Simply, everything that happens within the play. What happens to the characters, physically, emotionally, psychologically?

DRAMATURG   A theatre practitioner concerned with selecting plays for a theatre company, working with playwrights on the development of new scripts, and working with directors on research issues.

DRESSING THE SET   The placement of furniture and prop items on the raw set to provide mood and sense of identity.

DRESS REHEARSAL   A rehearsal that stimulates the conditions of public performance, with full costume, makeup, props, lights, etc.

DROP   A flat curtain, often painted, that is suspended from the flies.

ECCYCLEMA   In classical Greek tragedy, a wheeled vehicle or movable platform on which was depicted events and actions that took place off stage.

ELIZABETHAN TRAGEDY   Often Senecan in nature, the tragedies depart from the strictures of Aristotle as to unities and character. For example, the protagonist of *Macbeth* is not so much a good man with a tragic flaw as a potentially great man who uses his gifts for evil purposes. *(Macbeth, Hamlet,* etc. *)*

ENSEMBLE   A group of actors who work closely together and share the responsibility for the performance of a play.

EPIC DRAMA   A term used by Bertolt Brecht (and Erwin Piscator). Brecht called all drama preceding his own "Aristotelian," and described his own plays as seeking to arouse the spectator's intelligence by creating emotional distance.

EPIC THEATRE   Narrating a story on the stage by "dialecticizing" its events.

Brecht: The spectator of the dramatic theatre says: "Yes, I have felt the same. I am just like this. This is only natural. It will always be like this. This human being's suffering moves me, because there is no way out for him. This is great art: it bears the mark of the inevitable. I am weeping with those who weep on the stage, laughing with those who laugh."

Brecht: The spectator of the epic theatre says: "I should never have thought so. That is not the way to do it. This is most surprising, hardly creditable. This will have to stop. This human being's suffering moves me, because there would have been a way out for him. This is great: nothing here seems inevitable. I am laughing about those who weep on the stage, weeping about those who laugh."

Traditional theatre derives actions from the nature of the characters; epic theatre derives characters from their actions. The study of human nature is replaced by the study of human relations. (*Short Organum*)

EXODOS   In classical Greek tragedy, the final exit of the Chorus.

EXPRESSIONISM   A theatrical style that uses exaggeration and distortion in both design and acting to reflect the interior world of the characters.

EXTERNAL ACTING APPROACH   An acting approach that begins with text and movement rather than the psychological analysis of character.

FARCE   A mode of comedy that usually contains one-dimensional characters who are involved in outlandish situations. The normal laws of probability have no effect in farce, and there is a maximum of boisterous physical action. (*The Farce of Master Pierre Pathelin*)

FLAT   A piece of scenery built out of wood and muslin or canvas. Used to create walls or to back a set.

FLIES   The area above the stage where borders, drops, and scenery are hung.

FLOOR PLAN   A plan that shows, from a point of view above the set, the location of walls, doors, windows, and furniture. Often called ground plan.

FLY   To raise scenery items off the floor of the stage and out of view of the audience, in most cases, via lines run from the grid.

FORESTAGE   That part of the stage nearest the audience. Sometimes used interchangeably with "apron."

FOURTH WALL   The imaginary wall at the proscenium opening, "through" which the audience views the play.

FREEZE   In acting, to stand absolutely still for an agreed upon number of counts, or until curtain or blackout. Used for tableaux.

FRENCH CLASSICAL TRAGEDY Seventeenth-century neo-classical tragedy that strictly followed the French interpretation of Aristotle. *(Phaedra)*

GERMAN EXPRESSIONISM An artistic movement ("cry for freedom") in the visual and performing arts that prevailed in Germany from 1905 to 1922; it merged aesthetic and political views. In expressionist drama "humans are nothing but spirit and soul (...). Ecstatic and raving, they step out of the terrestrial thicket and yet are gifted with the true mark of humanity." (Kornfeld) It was generally done in lyrical-monologue style and distanced itself from the broad personal human spectrum which it found in naturalism with its imitating style.
Revolutionized the 20th century theatre because of its uncompromising demands and extreme experimentations (mechanical movements, the face as mask, a rhetoric of gesture, vocal work to approximate the range and variety of music). Most known playwrights are Georg Kaiser (*From Morn to Midnigh, Gas Trilogy*) and Ernst Toller (*Transfiguration, Man and Masses*).

GESTUS The term, English *gest*, derives from the theatre (gesture proper) and contains its opposite, *gist*, belonging to the discourse of law (grounds for action in a suit). Brecht's central artistic principal weaves the two together: the discourse of the body and the discourse of law. Basic attitudes (German *Haltungen*) of human beings are expressed by Gestus, not only gestures, but all outward signs of social/human relationships "deportment, voice intonation, facial expression." And "the clear and stylized expression of the social behavior of human beings towards each other."
Each scene has a Grundgestus, basic gestus. Conveyed in dialog and speech, gestische Sprache. For each character, a gestus — physical — which could be "quoted" like a line of dialog.

John Willet: "(Brecht's) conception of the 'Gestus' ... closely akin ... to Behaviorism is a central part of his doctrine, but it is hard to make it so in English, for there is no single word by which 'Gestus' can be translated. It is at once gesture and gist, attitude and point; one aspect of the relation between two people, studied singly, cut to essentials and physically or verbally expressed. It excludes the psychological, the subconscious, the metaphysical unless they can be conveyed in concrete terms. 'All feelings must be externalized,' Brecht later wrote."

GOBO A stencil placed inside a lighting instrument to create a pattern of reflected light on the floor or on a cyclorama or scenic unit.

GRAND DRAPE   A curtain that hangs from the top of the proscenium arch and that is often drawn back and tied at the sides to decorate the proscenium opening.

GRIDIRON (GRID)   A framework, usually of steel, above the stage area. Used to support flown scenery.

GROUND CLOTH   Waterproof canvas that is used to cover the stage floor.

GROUNDLINGS   In Elizabethan theatre, those persons who stood in the yard (pit).

GROUND PLAN   A plan that shows, from a point of view above the set, the location of walls, doors, windows, and furniture. Often called the floor plan evolves through collaboration by the scene designer and the director.

HAMARTIA   In classical Greek theatre, the "tragic flaw" or weakness of character in the protagonist that provoked the tragic action.

HAPPENING   A semi-dramatic event, often taking place outdoors, that is a planned reality involving the audience in the action.

HEROIC DRAMA   Primarily drama of the English Restoration period. Such plays are epic in scope and length, with love and valor as their subject, written in an elevated style, with the fate of empires hanging on the action. *(Conquest of Granada)*

HUBRIS   In classical Greek tragedy, the sin of excess that caused pride and arrogance.

IMPROVISATION   The spontaneous invention of actors used to explore text, character, or situation; a tool used by actors to freely create actions and language. Improvisation can be used in either rehearsal or performance.

INNER MONOLOGUE   The unspoken thoughts that accompany an actor's lines in method acting. The actor responds to the character's situation with a stream of spontaneous thoughts as if the actor were in the character's place.

INGÉNUE   The actress who plays the role of an innocent and attractive young woman.

INNER STAGE   In Elizabethan theatre, the recessed area (the alcove) directly behind the thrust stage.

INTERNAL ACTING APPROACH   An acting approach that is based on a psychological investigation of character and actor identification with character; involves imaging character history and placing oneself in the character's position.

JESSNER STAIRCASE   The German director Leopold Jessner was one of the first to use expressionist principles of concentration, scenic reduction, and dynamic acceleration. His 1919 production of Schiller's *Wilhelm Tell* on a staircase and his 1920 production of Shakespeare's *Richard III* on a similar terraced stage became famous for integrating an architectural element of design into the expression of the fateful course of events.

JUVENILE   The male equivalent of the ingénue.

KABUKI   A popular Japanese theatre form that began in the sixteenth century; highly stylized with elaborate action, exaggerated gestures and speech patterns, and magnificent costumes, make-up, and wigs.

KACHINA CYCLE   A sequence of ritual ceremonies performed by the Hopi people of the American Southwest that promotes the welfare of their community. The kachinas are the guardian spirits of the Hopi, who believe that the kachinas participate with them in dramatic ceremonies performed to ensure the success of the harvest and to preserve the Hopi way of life.

KATHAKALI   A form of dance drama from southern India in which the actors express a story through movement and complex hand gestures accompanied by musicians and singers who communicate the text. The actors play character types as in the Beijing Opera and spend years in intense training to perfect the strenuous and complicated movement skills. The dramas themselves are based on the *Ramayana* and the *Mahabbarata*, two epic Sanskrit poems.

KUROKO   A performer dressed in black (with a hood) in the tradition of the kabuki theatre; changes scenery and props and helps actors with onstage costume changes.

KOMMOS   A responsive lyric between Chorus and actors in classical Greek tragedy.

LIGHT LEAK   Light that inadvertently shows through a crack or seam in a set.

LIGHT PLOT   A diagram that shows the position and type of each lighting instrument to be used for a given production. The diagram is used as a tool in discussions between the lighting designer and the director and is also used by the technicians who hang the lights in the theatre.

LIGHT SPILL   Light that strikes the proscenium arch or some area of the set and then "spills" off onto the stage.

MASK   A fundamental device for establishing character that has been used in dramatic presentations throughout the world since the beginning of theatre.

THE MEININGER   Georg II, duke of Saxony-Meiningen, opened the 1866 season of his theatre with *Hamlet*, a production, which challenged fundamentally the perception of Shakespeare on German and wider Middle European stages. His idea of ensemble work, a well-balanced, dedicated and compatible artistic team became a model. Artfully prepared crowd scenes became a hallmark of Meininger productions. As a skilled draftsman, the duke worked for aesthetically pleasing stage pictures with actors arranged asymmetrically for conscious effects of line and mass. He sketched stage compositions, blocking diagrams, and set and costume designs. Historically accurate sets and costumes, long and disciplined rehearsals, scenes tried in a variety of interpretations until the artistically correct one had been found, actors were coached on the emphasis or volume of single lines and words, props were used from the first rehearsal. In 1874 the first tour of the Meininger with six productions to Berlin. The opening performance of *Julius Caesar* has been credited with changing the course of German and European theatre history.

MELODRAMA   Plays (originally with music) in which protagonists are totally pure, antagonists are totally evil, and both dramatic action and characterization are sacrificed to violent effect. Such plays end with exact demonstrations of poetic justice.

METHOD ACTING   An internal approach to acting used in the United States (developed by Lee Strasberg) that was influenced by the work of Konstantin Stanislavsky. Method acting uses a close study of character psychology to determine the character's sequence of intentions or objectives. Method acting also relies on the actor's own life experiences as a major source of material for character creation. Helped actors of silent movies to adapt their craft to the demands of motion pictures.

MIME   A performer who seeks to express the dramatic through body movement, without vocal accompaniment; unlike with dance, the movement is not keyed to music.

MIRACLE PLAYS   Often difficult if not impossible to distinguish from mystery plays, these are Medieval verse dramas that take their plots from Biblical history or the legends of the saints. Some critics insist that this category includes only plays based on the lives of the saints.

MISE-EN-SCENE   The total physical environment of a play (sets, costumes, movement, etc.)

MONOLOGUE   Related to the soliloquy, this form of stage address is delivered by a character who is usually (though not always) alone on stage. The material does not represent that character's thoughts, however, but is clearly material the character wishes to communicate, primarily to the audience.

MOOD (ATMOSPHERE)   The prevailing emotional context of the play.

MORALITY PLAY   A Medieval play allegorically presenting the Christian way of life by having the characters represent the virtues and vices struggling for the soul of Man. In later plays, primarily in the Tudor and Renaissance periods, the format of the morality was adapted to teach things other than Christianity. *(Everyman)*

MOSCOW ART THEATRE   Established by Konstantin Stanislavsky and Vladimir Nemirovich-Danchenko in 1898, this theatre and its practices, especially those of Stanislavsky, exerted great influence on the development of Western theatre practice in the first half of the 20th century.

MYSTERY PLAY   A Medieval style of Verse drama, taking its plots from incidents in the Old and New Testaments. *(Noah, Second Shepherd's Play)*

NATURALISTIC DRAMA   A form of dramatic realism, based primarily on social Darwinism, which shows middle- and lower-class characters being shaped by their environment. Promoted by the Freie Bühne (Free Stage), founded in 1889 by a group of young Berlin intellectuals, to establish naturalist production methods and, as a private subscription theatre, to provide a venue for plays that were banned from the public stage. Most influential Gerhart Hautpmann *(Before Sunrise, The Weavers)*. Although naturalism held the stage no more than a decade its influence on theatrical practice was seminal and lasting all over the Western world.

OFF BOOK Memorizing your lines so you can perform without the script. During the period immediately after going off book, it is expected that you will have to be prompted (call for lines), and you should do so without apology so that you do not lose concentration or your sense of action.

ORCHESTRA   In classical Greek theatre, the circular "dancing place" in front of the scene house. In the Hellenistic theatre the circle was cut to a half-circle. Today the term is used to designate the area immediately in front of the stage.

OUTER STAGE   The forestage or thrust stage of the Elizabethan theatre. This is where most of the dramatic action took place.

PAGEANT WAGONS   In Medieval Europe (mostly England, Spain and Germany), these were wagons containing a curtained playing area, set, and technical equipment necessary for staging a play. The exact structure is still debated.

PARABASIS   In Greek Old Comedy, the coming forward of the Chorus to address the audience and promote the playwright's views.

PAPERING THE HOUSE   A term referring to the practice of issuing large quantities of complimentary tickets, or selling large numbers of tickets at reduced prices, in order to secure a large audience.

PARADOS   In the classical Greek theatre, a passageway through which the Chorus entered the orchestra. Also, the opening choral dance.

PERIPETIA (PERIPETY)   In classical Greek tragedy, a reversal of circumstances. Usually, a reversal in the fortunes of the hero of the play.

PLOT   The sequence of actions that determines what happens in a play; the events that make up the play's story.

POOR THEATRE   A term used by Polish director Jerzy Grotowski to identify theatre that uses only those materials necessary to extend the expression of the actor. At the Polish Laboratory Theatre, scenery and costumes were made of the simplest, least costly materials, and no scenic elements were used merely to provide background or ornamentation.

PRESENTATIONAL STAGING   Staging that makes obvious use of the theatre's resources.

PREVIEW   A performance that is present to an invited audience or at a reduced ticket price to allow actors to work in front of an audience before the official opening of a play.

PROJECT (PROJECTION) Usually referring to the voice, this term means increasing audibility so that the actor can be heard at the rear of the house. The term is also, though less often, properly applied to stage movement and gesture, which must be enlarged in proportion so that it "projects" visibly to the rear of the house.

PROLOGUE In classical Greek theatre, the action before the entry of the Chorus. In later theatre the introduction to the play.

PROMPT BOOK The copy of the script kept by the stage manager that contains the blocking, the lighting and sound cues, and all the rest of the physical aspects of a production. It is possible to re-create a production from the prompt book, and this is sometimes done in the case of great European productions. Some of Shakespeare's plays were printed from his prompt books. (In film, the script supervisor keeps a book that records every shot and permits the editor to access particular takes in a scene.)

PROMPTING Giving the actor the line when he or she asks for it, usually by calling "line." Prompter is a profession in European Theatre during rehearsals and performances. In the US prompting is done by the stage manager in the theater and only during the rehearsals.

PROP Anything your character handles. In theater, it is wise to begin working with rehearsal substitutes as soon as you are off book.

PROSCENIUM The wall separating the audience from backstage. In classical Greek theatre the front wall of the stagehouse.

PROSCENIUM ARCH The opening in the proscenium wall through which the audience views the stage.

PROTAGONIST From classical Greek theatre, the leading character in a play; the character for whom the audience has the most sympathy and in whom they are most interested.

RAKE To slant the stage floor up from front to back. Sometimes used to identify an auditorium in which the house floor is slanted up from the first row of seats to the back of the auditorium.

REALISM A theatrical style that creates an illusion of daily life through the presentation of a detailed environment, natural actions, and language that sounds as if it were overheard in ordinary circumstances.

REHEARSAL The process of exploration and repetition used to prepare a play for public presentation.

REHEARSAL COSTUME A temporary costume worn during rehearsal to give the actor the opportunity to construct character in response to physical costume restrictions and the psychological dimensions of the costume.

REPERTOIRE (REPERTORY) A selection of plays or roles that a performer or a performing troupe has perfected and is prepared to present.

REPERTORY COMPANY A theatrical company that performs, in some method of rotation, the works in their repertoire.

RESOLUTION That point in the play when the conflicts are resolved. Also, the method used to solve the conflicts within the play.

RETURN A flat used at the right and left wings, which can run off stage behind the tormentor. Sometimes the flat (return) can serve as the tormentor.

ROMANTIC COMEDY A play in which the central plot concerns a love affair between a beautiful, idealized heroine and a handsome hero. The affair does not run smooth but ends well. (*As You Like It* or *Twelfth Night*)

SATIRIC COMEDY Plays that ridicule, for a corrective purpose, violations of moral or social standards. (*Lysistrata* or *Volpone*)

SCENARIO The written prose plot and description of events for a play or performance. For playwrights, the first step (prose outline) in creating a play. In *commedia*, the material from which the performers worked onstage. Today also called a breakdown (of the beats of a scene).

SCENE 1. The smaller units that make up the acts in a play. 2. A particular moment in the performance of a play. 3. The arrangement of the scene design elements. 4. In some older plays, scenes are marked by the entrance of major characters; there are called French scenes.

SCENE DESIGNER The theatre artist responsible for interpreting plays through shaping and defining the stage space.

SCENOGRAPHY The work of the scene designer or combined work of the scene designer, costume designer, lighting designer, and sound designer, also known as stage design.

SCRIPT The dialogue, stage directions, and character descriptions that together constitute the printed text of a play.

SENECAN TRAGEY Tragic drama based on the formulas of the Roman tragic dramatist Seneca. These include revenge, adultery, incest, murder, mutilation, torture, and general carnage. *(Thyestes, The Spanish Tragedy)*

SET PIECES Scenery that is capable of standing without support, or that has some form of acceptable support built into it, such as door frames, window frames, etc. Often used in nonrealistic productions.

SETTING The locale and period in which a drama takes place, or, more practically, the scenery, props, and costumes used in its staging.

SKELETON SET The rudiments or bare essentials of a set that are used to provoke the imagination of the audience. Usually made up of "set pieces."

SKENE Originally a small hut behind the orchestra of the classical Greek theatre, used for costume changes. Eventually this became an elaborate building, with its façade used to provide a "set." Its popularity in classical theatre has led to the English term "scene."

SKY-DROP A large fabric drop painted to represent the blue sky and used to mask the backstage area. Sometimes, though not always, the sky-drop is the same as the cyclorama.

SOCIALIST REALISM A form of realistic theatre produced in the former Soviet Union, presenting an idealized view of life under Communism; heavily influenced by government manipulation.

SOLILOQUY A speech delivered by an actor alone onstage, which by convention is understood by the audience to be not a part of the dialogue, but the character's internal thoughts.

STAGE DIRECTIONS The indications in a script about the character's gestures, tone of voice, and so on, such as *(he moves away angrily)*. Some teachers and directors tell actors to ignore stage directions because in some so-called acting versions of a play these may have been inserted not by the writer by from the prompt book of an earlier production. However, many writers provide stage directions, and you should consider them for the information they contain about the behavior and emotions of your character, even if that behavior eventually takes a different form in your particular production.

STAGE FRIGHT   Everyone gets it. The only antidote is to be fully focused on the task at hand, and passionately committed to it.

STAGE LEFT   The left side of the stage from the actor's point of view.

STAGE RIGHT   The right side of the stage from the actor's point of view.

STASIMON   In classical Greek theatre, a choral ode sung and danced after the chorus enters the orchestra.

STROPHE   A movement or division of the choral ode.

STOCK (STOCK COMPANY)   A resident acting company that presents a series of plays for limited runs, but not brought back as in repertory.

STOCK CHARACTERS   Character types that regularly occur in certain types of drama: Greek New Comedy and Roman comedy provided later drama with most of these characters, such as the prostitute, parasite, and miser; the *commedia* provide such characters as Arlecchino, Pantalone, and Zanni; more recent stock characters are the stage Irishman, Englishman, Scotsman, and the down-east Yankee.

SUBTEXT   After Stanislavsky, the thoughts and feelings of the character that are unspoken but expressed through gesture, facial expressions, and phrasing.

SUPER-OBJECTIVE   In scoring a role, the overall objective of any character in a play.

TABLE READING   Usually the first rehearsal of a script in which the actors literally sit at a table and read it aloud. During any reading, it is important that the actors try to play in relationship and experience the action of the scene, and not fall into a flat, "literary" tone.

TABLEAU   Often used in melodrama, the actors "freeze" at certain points where the stage picture has artistic visual values, or where the director wishes to emphasize certain emotional situations. In many cases the tableau comes at the end of an act, on the curtain line, and is held until the curtain falls.

TEASER   A border that is just upstage behind the front curtain. It masks the flies and may be used to adjust the effective height of the proscenium opening.

TECHNICAL REHEARSAL   In theater, the rehearsal in which the lighting, sound, and nearly completed set are first brought together under the command of the stage manager. At the technical rehearsal, the lighting and soundboard operators have their first chance to rehearse their cues, and the designers are seeing the set and props in action. Great patience is required of the actors at a "tech" rehearsal, which is sometimes quite lengthy.

THEATRE OF THE ABSURD   Plays that focus on the lack of meaning in human existence, such as those written by Samuel Beckett, Eugene Ionesco, and Jean Genet.

THEATRICAL CONVENTIONS   Elements of dramatic construction and performance accepted by theatre practitioners and audience members in a given community that facilitate the presentation of plays. Conventions of the Greek theatre include masked actors and offstage violence.

THEATRE-IN-THE-ROUND   Theatre in which the audience surrounds the action of the play. Often called "arena staging."

THEATRON   In classical Greek theatre, the place where the audience sat.

THEOLOGEION   In classical Greek theatre, a high platform from which the gods and heroes spoke.

THESPIAN   A term used for "actor" taken from the name of Thespis, the first recognized Greek actor.

THRUST STAGE   A stage with a projected apron or playing area that allows the audience to view the action from three sides.

THYMELE   In classical Greek theatre the altar of Dionysus, which stood in the center of the orchestra.

TORMENTORS   Flats at the right and left wing areas, close to the proscenium opening, that help mask the backstage area.

TOTAL THEATRE   A theatrical style that integrates sound, words, movement, lights, music, and color to create a performance that emphasizes gesture and imagery as much or more than language.

TRAGEDY   The dramatic genre initiated by ancient Greek playwrights such as Aeschylus, Sophocles, and Euripides. Tragedy focuses on suffering and loss but celebrates the will of the individual to choose his or her own course of action.

TRAGICOMEDY   A play in which the action is serious and seems to threaten disaster to the protagonist but ends with a happy reversal. *(Merchant of Venice)*

TRAP   An opening in the stage floor; usually covered by a trapdoor, that permits entrances and exits from below stage.

TRAVELER   A slotted track used to hang a draw curtain.

TYPE-CASTING   Casting an actor on the basis that his age, size, physical appearance, personality, and, in some cases, nature and metabolism resemble those of the character he is to portray.

UNIT SET   A set consisting of various pieces of scenery that are designed to fit together in several combinations to shift the scene.

UPSTAGE   The back of the stage. For many years, stages were raked-that is, they slanted up toward the back to provide the audience a better view. Thus, when an actor moved toward the back of the stage he moved up in height.

VAUDEVILLE   From the French, *chanson du vau de vire*, this originally meant a lightweight theatrical work interspersed with songs and dances. Later understanding was a production of several acts, including songs, dances, monologues, etc., which were essentially unrelated but offered a variety of entertainment. Popular in the United States throughout the early 1930's, Vaudeville still exists in England under the title of "Music Hall."

VERB   The verb phrase that succinctly describes your action at a given moment, such as "to persuade." Only transitive verbs are used, and all forms of the verb "to be" (such as "being angry" or "being a victim") are avoided.

VERFREMDUNGSEFFEKT (V-EFFECT) or ALIENATION EFFECT (A-EFFECT)   To distance, alienate, to destroy illusion, identification. Allow pleasure of discovery, understanding, audience for the age of science — Newton and apple.

Hegel: "The known, because it is know, is the unknown."

Brecht: "Alientation (or Estrangement) of an incident or character simply means taking from that incident or character that which is self-evident, known, or obvious, and arousing about them wonder or curiosity."

Brecht: "Have you ever looked at your watch closely? He who asks that question knows that I've looked at my watch quite frequently; but with this question he withdraws from me that which is habitual, that which has nothing to say to me."

WELL-MADE-PLAY Based primarily on the works of Scribe and Sardou, this means a play that follows a certain set pattern in its construction-that is, a three-act structure that emphasizes popular stock scenes and devices and that neatly resolves all plot elements.

WINGS The offstage space on the left and right of the playing area. Sometimes this term is used also to refer to wing pieces or flats which are used at the left and right edges of the playing area.

40 Important Plays

Major playwrights from different national dramas, assigned to be read in depth, are marked in **bold** typeface. Awareness of the progression of the art of these individual masters as well as of their period is expected from graduate students and professionals.

Ancient Greece and Rome

Aeschylus	*The Oresteia*	458 BC
	Prometheus Bound	456 BC
Sophocles	*Antigone*	422 BC
	Oedipus Rex	426 BC
	Oedipus at Colonus	406 BC
Euripides	*Medea*	431 BC
	Cyclops	425 BC
	The Trojan Women	415 BC
	Orestes	408 BC
	The Bacchae	408 BC

Aristophanes	*The Birds*	414 BC
	The Frogs	405 BC
Menander	*The Grouch*	320 BC
Plautus	*The Twin Menaechmi*	205 BC
Terence	*The Brothers*	160 BC
Seneca	*Medea*	50 AD

Medieval England and Europe

	The Wakefield Creation	1350–1450
	The Murder of Abel	
	Noah and His Sons	
	Abraham and Isaac	
	The Death of Herod	
	The Cornwall Death of Pilate	
	The Second Shepherd's Play	
	Everyman	1500

Renaissance Italy

| Machiavelli | *The Mandrake* | 1520 |

Renaissance Spain

Lope de Vega	*Fuente Ovejuna*	1619
Tirso de Molina	*The Trickster of Seville*	1630
Calderon de Barca	*Life is a Dream*	1635

Renaissance England

Marlowe	*Dr. Faustus*	1588
Shakespeare	*Romeo & Juliet*	1594
	Richard II	1595
	Henry IV, Part I	1597
	As You Like It	1599
	Hamlet	1600
	Othello	1604
	King Lear	1605
	Macbeth	1605
	Antony & Cleopatra	1606
	The Tempest	1611
Dekker	*The Shoemaker's Holiday*	1600
Jonson	*Volpone*	1606
Tourneur	*The Revenger's Tragedy*	1607
Beaumont & Fletcher	*The Knight of the Burning Pestle*	1607
Webster	*The Duchess of Malfi*	1612
Middleton & Rowley	*The Changeling*	1624

Restoration & Eighteenth Century England

Villiers	*The Rehearsal*	1671
Wycherly	*The Country Wife*	1673
Congreve	*The Way of the World*	1700
Steele	*The Conscious Lovers*	1722
Gay	*The Beggar's Opera*	1728
Lillo	*The London Merchant*	1731
Goldsmith	*She Stoops to Conquer*	1773
Sheridan	*The Rivals*	1775
	The School for Scandal	1777

Nineteenth Century England

Wilde	*Importance of Being Earnest*	1895
Shaw	*Man & Superman*	1903
	Major Barbara	1905
	Heartbreak House	1914
	Saint Joan	1923

Seventeenth Century/Eighteenth Century France and Italy

Corneille	*The Cid*	1636
Racine	*Phaedre*	1677
Moliere	*School for Wives*	1663
	Critique/School for Wives	1663
	The Rehearsal of Versailles	1663
	The Misanthrope	1666
	The Miser	1668
	Tartuffe	1669

Nineteenth Century France

Hugo	*Hernani*	1830
De Musset	*Lorenzaccio*	1833
Dumas	*Camille*	1852
Sardou	*A Scrap of Paper*	1860
Zola	*Therese Raquin*	1873
Maeterlinck	*The Intruder*	1891
	Pelleas and Melisande	1892

Nineteenth Century Germany

Goethe	*Egmont*	1788
Schiller	*Maria Stuart*	1800
Goethe	*Faustus, Part One*	1808
Kleist	*Prince of Homburg*	1811
Buchner	*Danton's Death*	1833
	Woyzeck	1837
Wedekind	*Springs Awakening*	1892
Hauptmann	*The Weavers*	1892
Schnitzler	*La Ronde*	1900

Nineteenth Century Russia

Gogol	*The Inspector General*	1842
Chekhov	*The Seagull*	1896
	Uncle Vanya	1899
	The Three Sisters	1900
	The Cherry Orchard	1903
Tolstoy	*The Power of Darkness*	1889
Gorki	*The Lower Depths*	1903
Andreyev	*He Who Gets Slapped*	1916

Nineteenth Century Scandinavia

Strindberg	*Miss Julie*	1888
	The Ghost Sonata	1907
Ibsen	*Brand*	1866
	Peer Gynt	1867
	A Doll's House	1879
	Hedda Gabler	1890

| | *When We Dead Awaken* | 1899 |

Nineteenth Century America

| Herne | *Margaret Fleming* | 1890 |

Twentieth Century America

O'Neill	*The Emperor Jones*	1921
	Desire Under the Elms	1924
	Mourning Becomes Electra	1931
	Long Day's Journey Into Night	1941
	The Iceman Cometh	1946
Saroyan	*The Time of Your Life*	1939
Williams	*The Glass Menagerie*	1945
	A Streetcar Named Desire	1947
Miller	*Death of a Salesman*	1949
	The Crucible	1953
Albee	*Zoo Story*	1960
	Who's Afraid of Virginia Woolf?	1962
Jones	*Dutchman*	1964
Rabe	*The Basic Training of Pavlo Hummel*	1971
	Streamers	1976

Twentieth Century England

Eliot	*Murder in the Cathedral*	1935
Osborne	*Look Back in Anger*	1956
Pinter	*The Birthday Party*	1958
	The Caretaker	1960

	The Homecoming	1965
Stoppard	Rosencrantz & Guildenstern are Dead	1966
Bond	Saved	1965

Twentieth Century Europe

Jarry	Ubu Roi	1896
Synge	Riders to the Sea	1904
	Playboy of the Western World	1907
Kaiser	From Morn to Midnight	1916
Brecht	Baal	1918
	Threepenny Opera	1928
	The Good Woman of Setzuan	1938
	Mother Courage and Her Children	1941
	The Caucasian Chalk Circle	1944
Pirandello	Six Characters in Search of an Author	1921
	Henry IV	1922
O'Casey	Juno and the Paycock	1924
Cocteau	Orphee	1926
DeGhelderode	Pantagleize	1929
Lorca	Blood Wedding	1933
	The House of Bernardo Alba	1935
Sartre	No Exit	1944
Giradoux	The Madwoman of Chaillot	1945
Genet	The Maids	1947
	The Balcony	1956
	The Blacks	1959
Jonesco	The Bald Soprano	1949
	Rhinoceros	1960
Betti	The Queen and the Rebels	1951
Beckett	Waiting for Godot	1953
	Endgame	1957
Weiss	Marat Sade	1959

41 Reference List

Aristotle. *The Poetics*. Gateway, Chicago, 1961. Transl. Kenneth A. Telford.

Artaud, Antonin. *The Theatre and Its Double*. Grove Press, New York, 1958.

Bach, George. *Aggression Lab*. Kendall/Hunt, Dubuque, IA, 1971.

Bacon, Wallace A. and Breen, Robert S. *Literature as Experience*. McGraw-Hill, New York, 1959.

Barton, John. *Playing Shakespeare*. Methuen, London and New York, 1984.

Beckerman, Bernard. *Dynamics of Drama*. Drama Book Publishers, New York, 1979.

Brook, Peter. *The Empty Space*. Antheneum, New York, 1968.

Bullough, Edward. *Æsthetics: Lectures and essays*. Stanford University Press, Stanford, CA, 1957. Edited with an introd. by Elizabeth M. Wilkinson.

Campbell, Joseph. *The Masks of God*. Viking, New York, 1959.

Carney, Sean. *Brecht and Critical Theory*. Routledge, New York, 2005.

Cassirer, Ernst. *The philosophy of symbolic forms*. Yale University Press, New Haven, 1953. Transl. by Ralph Manheim. Pref. and introd. by Charles W. Hendel.

Cole, Toby and Chinoy, Helen Krich (editors). *Actors on acting: The theories, techniques, and practices of the great actors of all times as told in their own words*. Crown Publishers, New York, new rev. ed edn., 1970.

Dewey, John. *Experience and nature*. Open Court Publishing Company, Chicago, London, 1925.

Ernst, Earle. *The Kabuki Theatre.* Oxford University Press, New York, 1956.

Esslin, Martin. *Brecht: the man and his work.* Doubleday, Garden City, NY, 1960.

———. *Theatre of the Absurd.* Doubleday, Garden City, NY, 1961.

Gielgud, John. *An actor and his time.* Penguin Books, New York, 1981.

Grotowski, Jerzy. *Towards a Poor Theatre.* Methuen, London, 1969.

Guthrie, Tyrone. *Tyrone Guthrie on acting.* Viking, New York, 1971.

Hagen, Uta. *Respect for Acting.* Maxmillan, New York, 1973.

Hall, Edward. *The Silent Language.* Doubleday, Garden City, NY, 1959.

Hunningher, Benjamin. *The origin of the theater, an essay.* Hill and Wang, New York, 1961.

Jones, Frank Pierce. *Body awareness in action : a study of the Alexander technique.* Schocken Books, New York, 1976.

Leabhart, Thomas. *Etienne Decroux.* Routledge, New York, 2007.

Lessac, Arthur. *Body wisdom : the use and training of the human body.* Drama Book Specialists, New York, 1978.

Mamet, David. *Writing in Restaurants.* Viking, New York, 1986.

Meyerhold, Vsevolod Emilevich. *Meyerhold on theatre.* Hill and Wang, New York, 1969. Translated and edited with a critical commentary, by Edward Braun.

Olivier, Laurence. *Confessions of an Actor.* Simon & Schuster, New York, 1982.

Otto, Walter Friedrich. *Dionysus, myth and cult.* Indiana University Press, Bloomington, 1965. Transl. with an introd. by Robert B. Palmer.

Redgrave, Sir, Michael. *In My Mind's I: An actor's autobiography.* Viking Press, New York, 1983.

Rischbieter, Henning. *Art and the Stage in the 20ᵗʰ Century; painters and sculptors work for the theater.* New York Graphic Society, Greenwich, CT, 1968.

Sapir, Edward. *Language, an introduction to the study of speech.* Harcourt, Brace & World, New York, 1921.

Schechner, Richard. *Performance Theory.* Routledge, New York, 1988.

Schlauch, Margaret. *The Gift of Language.* Dover Publications, New York, 1955.

Stanislavski, Konstantin. *My Life in Art.* Theatre Arts Books, New York, 1952. Transl. J. J. Robbins.

Willet, John (editor). *Brecht on Theatre: The Development of an Aesthetic.* Methuen, London, England, 1964.

Wilsher, Toby. *The Mask Handbook.* Routledge, New York, 2006.

42 Bibliography

[1] Becket, *Waiting for Godot*, Faber and Faber, London, 1965.

[2] Bertolt Brecht, *Phasen einer Regie*, Theaterarbeit (Ruth Berlau and Helene Weigel, eds.), Dresdner Verlag, 1952.

[3] Bertolt Brecht, *The epic theatre*, Directors on Directing: A Source Book of the Modern Theatre (Toby Cole and Helen Krich Chinoy, eds.), Macmillan, New York, 1963, pp. 230–240.

[4] _____ , *Schriften zum Theater*, Gesammelte Werke in 20 Bänden, vol. IV, Suhrkamp, Frankfurt a. Main, 1967.

[5] William Browning, *Defining space and storytelling: Stage design for epic theatre*, [22].

[6] Albert Camus, *Lyrical and critical*, H. Hamilton, London, 1967, transl. Philip Thody.

[7] Marvin Carlson, *Theories of the theatre*, Cornell University Press, Ithaka and London, 1993.

[8] Richard A. Davison, *Notes on Heinz-Uwe Haus rehearsing Brecht's "Galileo"*, Communications (2007), no. 36.

[9] Kathleen Mary Doyle, *Dramaturging "Mother Courage and Her Children" in the United States and Germany*, Communications **24** (1995), no. 2, 23–29.

[10] Fritz Engels, *Bühnenrundschau*, Berliner Tageblatt (1919), no. 17.

[11] F. Scott Fitzgerald, *The short stories of F. Scott Fitzgerald*, Scribner, New York, 1989, Ed. Matthew J. Bruccoli.

[12] Otto Friedrich, *Before the deluge: A portrait of Berlin in the 1920s*, Harper & Row, New York, 1972.

[13] Jerzy Grotowski, *Towards a poor theatre*, Methuen, London, 1969.

[14] Willi Handl, Berliner Lokal-Anzeiger No 466, Oct 1 1919.

[15] O. B. Hardison, *Aristotle's Poetics; a translation and commentary for students of literature*, Prentice-Hall, Englewood Cliffs, NJ, 1968, transl. Leon Golden.

[16] Heinz-Uwe Haus, *Director's notes – Ui in Greece*, Communications **75** (1985), 14–15.

[17] ———, *On experimental theatre*, Gestus **2** (1986), no. 2, 138–140.

[18] ———, *Theatre as a transcultural event*, History of European Ideas **20** (1995), no. 1–3, 71–79.

[19] ———, *Learning "Fundamentals of Directing"*, Lo Straniero **32** (2000).

[20] ———, *Hubris and blindness: How much does Alan Greenspan matter*, Re-Reading Ancient Greek Theater Texts, Cyclos Theater Books, Nicosia, 2005.

[21] _____, *Generality is the enemy of children's theatre*, Epi Skinis (2006), no. 23, 13–14, in Greek.

[22] _____, *Notes on directing*, no. 477691, Lulu, 2007.

[23] Ernst Heilborn, Frankfurter Zeitung No 747, Oct 6 1919.

[24] Ernest Hemingway, *Monologue to the maestro: A high seas letter*, Scribner, New York, 1967, Ed. William White.

[25] Linda Henderson, *Music of the spheres: Singing actors in "The Life of Galileo"*, Communications (2007), no. 36.

[26] Frederick J. Hoffman, *Mortality and modern literature*, The Meaning of Death (Herman Feifel, ed.), McGraw-Hill, New York, 1959.

[27] Irving Louis Horowitz, *The struggle for democracy*, The National Interest **83** (2006).

[28] Herbert Ihering, Der Tag No 217, Oct 2 1919.

[29] _____, Vossische Zeitung No 609, Nov 29 1919.

[30] Sigfried Jacobsohn, Die Weltbühne No 42, Oct 9 1919.

[31] Leopold Jessner, *Schriften: Theater der zwanziger Jahre*, Henschelverlag Kunst u. Gesellschaft, Berlin, 1979.

[32] Paul Klee, *On modern art*, Faber & Faber, London, 1948.

[33] Franz Koeppen, Berliner Börsen-Zeitung No 495, Nov 13 1920.

[34] Panagiotis Kondylis, *Planetarische Politik nach dem Kalten Krieg*, Akademie Verlag, Berlin, 1992.

[35] Paul Kornfeld, *Theaterlexikon*, Weimar, 1932.

[36] Fritz Kortner, *Aller Tage Abend*, Kindler, München, 1959.

[37] Klaus Kändler (ed.), *Georg Kaiser, Werke in drei Bänden*, vol. 3, Aufbau Verlag, Berlin, 1979.

[38] Fred Lapisardi, *Staging yeats in the twenty-first century*, The Edwin Mellen Press, Lewinston, 2006.

[39] Felicia Hardison Londré, *The history of world theater: From the English Restoration to the present*, Continuum, New York, 1991.

[40] Georg Lukács, *Soul and form*, MIT Press, Cambridge, Mass., 1974, transl. Anna Bostock.

[41] *Bip – an obituary*, The Economist 384, Sep 27 2007.

[42] Vladimir Mayakovski, *Left march*, A Second Book of Russian Verse (C. M. Bowra, ed.), Macmillan, London, 1948.

[43] Moliere, *Werke*, Insel-Verlag, Leipzig, 1968.

[44] Robert O. Paxton, *Europe in the twentieth century*, Harcourt, New York, 1975.

[45] Alfred Polgar, Die Weltbühne No 3, Jan 19 1922.

[46] Bernhard Reich, *Community in classical athens*, lecture manuscript, Reich-Lacis-Archiv Berlin, 1927.

[47] Max Reinhardt, *Schriften*, Henschel, Berlin, 1974.

[48] Clifford A. Ridley, *'inherit the wind': A new production stirs excitement with stars, director*, Philadelphia Inquirer, April 8 1996, p. F6.

[49] Jean-Paul Sartre, *Sartre on theatre*, Pantheon Books, New York, 1976, transl. Frank Jellinck.

[50] Diether Schmidt (ed.), *Schriften deutscher Künstler des zwanzigsten Jahrhunderts*, VEB Verl. d. Kunst, Dresden, 1964.

[51] Anthony Charles H. Smith, *Orghast at persepolis*, Eyre Methuen, 1975.

[52] Ludwig Sternaux, Tägliche Rundschau No 495, Nov 13 1920.

[53] Studs Terkel, *The spectator: Talk about movies and people who make them*, New Press, New York, 1999.

[54] Thucydides, *The history of the Peloponnesian war*, Oxford and London, 1866.

[55] Vasily Osipovich Toporkov, *Stanislavski in rehearsal. The final years.*, Theatre Arts Books, New York, 1976.

[56] David Tracy, *Plurality and ambiguity: Hermeneutics, religion, hope*, Harper & Row, New York, 1987.

[57] Leon Trotzky, *Literature and revolution*, Russell & Russell, New York, 1957.

[58] John Willett (ed.), *Brecht on Theatre: The Development of an Aesthetic*, Hill and Wang, New York, 1989.

[59] Kurt Wolff, *Briefwechsel eines Verlegers*, Scheffler, Frankfurt am Main, 1966.

Short Biography

Heinz-Uwe Haus

Theatre director, Cultural Studies expert and Theatre scholar; since 1997 Professor at the Professional Theatre Training Program (PTTP) and the Theatre Department of the University of Delaware, Newark (USA).

Educated and trained in Germany at the Film Academy Potsdam- Babelsberg (Acting), as well as at the Humboldt Universität in Berlin (Cultural Studies, German Literature and Theatre Science).

Dr. Haus began his long artistic and academic career as director at the Deutsches Theater, Berlin, and founding member of the East Berlin Directing Institute. His productions include plays of the Ancient Greeks, Shakespeare, German classics, Brecht and the Expressionists, performed both in Germany and such countries as Canada, Cyprus, Finland, Greece, Italy, Turkey and the USA. Some of these productions have appeared in festivals throughout Europe.

Dr. Haus has been a guest professor at more than a dozen North American universities (such as NYU, Villanova, CSUN and the University of Washington) and has given more than 500 lectures and workshops worldwide. Besides publishing in his field, he writes about intercultural and political topics in German, English and Greek medias. He is Honorary Member of the Cyprus Centre of the International Theatre Institute and Honorary Citizen of the Greek community Catochi. In 2005 he received the Best Director Theatre Award THOC.

Dr. Haus was a board member of the East German "Democatic Awakening" party (Demokratischer Aufbruch) in 1989/90, and founder and representative of "The Praxis Group" in the US. 1992 – 1993 he worked as founding director of the Educational Centre Schloß Wendgräben of the Konrad-Adenauer-Foundation.

Dr. Haus co-founded in 1986 the International Workshop and Study Center for Ancient Greek Drama in Oeniades (Greece). From 2004 until 2007 he served as Academic Chair of the Institute for Ancient Greek Drama and Theatre in Droushia-Paphos (Cyprus). He has chaired the Intercultural group of ISSEI since 1994 and since 1996 has been a member of its Executive Committee.

Recent books of or about the author (in English)

Heinz-Uwe Haus, *(Re-Reading) Ancient greek theater texts*, second edition 2006 ed., Cyclos Theater Books, Nicosia, Cyprus, 2005, ISBN 9963-9164-0-6.

_____ , *Notes on directing*, Cyclos Theater Books, Nicosia, Cyprus, 2007, ISBN 978-9963-9164-3-6, a revised edition is available through `http://books.lulu.com/content/477691`.

Daniel Meyer-Dinkgräfe (ed.), *Brechtian theatre of contradictions: Providing moral strength under conditions of dictatorship: A Festschrift for Heinz-Uwe Haus*, Cambridge Scholars Publishing, Newcastle, UK, 2007, ISBN 978-1847184252.

Daniel Meyer-Dinkgräfe (ed.), *Views, positions, legacies: Interviews with German and British theatre artists, 1985-2007*, Cambridge Scholars Publishing, Newcastle, UK, 2007, ISBN-13: 978-1847182944.